The Golden Goose Ate All
The Grassroots

The Golden Goose Ate All The Grassroots

So, You Want To Go To Congress

By Jim Jacobs

Writers Club Press

San Jose New York Lincoln Shanghai

The Golden Goose Ate All The Grassroots
So, You Want To Go To Congress

Writers Club Press
an imprint of iUniverse, Inc.

For information address:
iUniverse, Inc.
5220 S. 16th St., Suite 200
Lincoln, NE 68512
www.iuniverse.com

The book is a fairly serious political work that should be read by anyone even thinking about running for public office, written in a humorous, and even ribald manner. Politics and Humor are such a dichotomy that it doesn't fit library classifications. Help!!

ISBN: 0-595-23528-X

Printed in the United States of America

To all of my Eagles, and to my niece, Ellen Sykes who has her own story to tell.

Jim Jacobs

Contents

1

FROM LITTLE ACORNS SPRING...

Running for the United States Congress is like a honeymoon. There are lots of surprises, you learn something new everyday, and all the while you are continually being *fucked.* Having said that let me hasten to add that this book is not about the negative aspects of running for office. But the statement is still a truism. On balance, the six months leading up to and including the election in which I ran embraced perhaps some of the most rewarding experiences of my life. So much so that I started out to share the experience with friends and family, who were not around to share in it with me. Halfway into the project, I decided that the story might have mass appeal to more than just friends and family and might even inspire a reader to do what I did and take on the world, or at least a good chunk of South Florida.

I want to describe to you when the first twinges of running for political office jogged a few of my brain cells, what made the idea grow, and the circumstances that even made it possible to take the better part of a year out of my life and take a shot at a job that 99.99% of the qualified people in this country wouldn't touch with a cattle prod. I will also share with you a phenomenon that still has me shaking my head in wonderment; how deceptively *easy* it was to become a political candidate and the Republican nominee for national office.

I also must caution, should you have any such aspirations, please do not consider this work as intended to be a primer on how to mount and conduct a political campaign. Remember one thing: *I lost!* Furthermore, I probably broke every accepted rule in the book in this shortest of all possible political careers, but I also generated over 86,000 votes, enough to get me elected in a lot of congressional districts around the country; not too shabby for not only a political unknown, but an unknown, period, with no money, no name recognition, no political base whatsoever, and in many situations, no idea of what I was doing. Nevertheless, this book should be required reading for *any* first time political candidate contemplating running for any elected office in this country. It should also be entertaining reading for anyone even vaguely interested in the political process because it will take you step by step through what it takes, not only to mount a political campaign, but to survive it. Finally, this book will be educational for anyone who would just like to become more knowledgeable about the political process.

Every publisher who rejected this book did so because they felt that it was too "regional" and would only sell well in South Florida. Yes, the events as described did take place in South Florida, but they could just as well have taken place anywhere. Every story ever told takes place *somewhere.* There were over 500 similar stories in the 1996 general election with over 1000 principal characters. I was but one of these and this is my story. What follows is the way I chose to tell it.

There are factors in my background, having nothing whatsoever to do with politics, which invariably led me to do what I did. In this chapter, I want to take you through a few incidents that shaped me as a person, defined the career path I would take, far from politics, and including a couple of career scenarios that even prepared me for such a departure from my "real world" pursuits in the technical and business world. This is not an autobiography, but it *is* an autobiography of a particular event, and should be taken as such. The significance of the material in this chapter will become much more obvious as the story unfolds. In the final chapters, the autobiographical aspects will give weigh to implications beyond the individual story, and transcend to a first-person account of some of the things that are wrong with our political system in general, as viewed by one who has been there, done that. *That* valued reader is the context of this book. And...you will find no sour grapes crushed between these covers.

To get where we need to go, it might help if you knew a little about me, and the kind of person I am, or think I am. At one time during the campaign a panelist on a candidate forum asked me what kind of person I would like to be if I could be anybody in the world. Being primed for an "issue" question, this one caught me totally off guard. However, I could not have lived the life I have led, with as little raw talent as I possess, without at least being somewhat quick on my feet. My answer, once I regained some semblance of composure was, "I guess I would like to be the person my dog thinks I am."

Off-the-wall, but it got me through the question and even garnered a sprinkling of spontaneous applause, something seldom heard outside the highly structured and professionally choreographed political debates you are accustomed to seeing on national TV.

Nevertheless, falling considerably short of my dog's image of me, I will admit to possessing an "A" type personality. Probably as good a place as any to start would be in the second grade, at Anna B. Lacey Elementary School, in Chattanooga, Tennessee. I was recently rummaging through some personal effects of my deceased mother when I came across a letter to my parents from my second grade teacher. The year was 1942. I will quote it in its entirety

---

"Dear Mr. and Mrs. Jacobs,

James has been a fine pupil throughout the year. He does excellent work in reading, spelling, writing, and numbers.

James has an aggressive personality. He can hold his own with anybody, anywhere, I believe. Though this trait is a good one in many ways, he is really too sure of himself. But, certainly, he is never shy, and he seems to have many friends.

James is promoted to third grade, Room 6.

/s/ Roberta Robinson   (over)

159 days present
14 days absent
3 days off roll"

It appears I had trouble getting to school, even then.

In what was then called Junior High School, I was heavily into sports: basketball and baseball being my two best. However, in those wonderful days before *Game Boy* and at that age one was expected to "go out" for *every* sport. Between football and basketball season there was a lull, and our coach devised a "Silver Gloves" intramural boxing tournament. All the "jocks" were expected to participate. Unfortunately, I did sufficiently well enough that the coach talked a few of us into fighting in the Golden Gloves in the novice division. This was not one of my better thought out decisions. I managed to win my first bout, and on the second night I drew a 20-something U.S. Army soldier from Puerto Rico in the 92 lb. weight division. He was a man, and I was a boy. Mercifully, the ref stopped it early in the second round, but that was the worst beating I ever received in my life. It must have been about this time that I decided that I'd better become a lover because I sure as hell wasn't a fighter. I also resolved that nobody was ever going to beat me like that ever again.

In 1949, my family moved to Montgomery, Alabama, and I still claim Alabama as my "home of record". I was still into sports, but I was also probably the worst student ever to graduate from Sidney Lanier High School, even losing my eligibility to play varsity sports in my junior year. I started out every morning, but I only made it all the way to school about three days a week, there being a couple of pool halls between where I lived and the high school. I shot a good stick then, and still do. However, that wasn't my only distraction. I was in love with a saucy little thing who eventually wound up with my cherry. Even then, I could be had, but I "weren't no pushover". The problem was that she rode to school with me and she wasn't any more inclined to go to school than I was. Plus, both our parents worked and there was no one at home all day at either house. Ah, life was good.

I was also immersed in a high school fraternity, the Commodores, about which you will hear more as this story unfolds. High school fraternities were not sanctioned by the schools, and for good reason. Looking back, I think our charter was to see who could drink the most beer, raise the most hell, and get into the most trouble. In that regard, the Commodores excelled.

Somewhere in there, my true love decided I was never going to amount to much, so she eloped with a motorcycle cop. Concurrently, a judge decided that my souped-up '41 Ford coupe and I were non-coexistial with the other citizens on the highways and byways, not to mention the city streets of the Great State of Alabama. He lifted my driver's license *for life*. Teenagers without wheels in the drive-in, making-out-on-lovers lane days of the early 1950s had a dismal social expectancy. It is truly amazing how a lack of alternatives tends to clear the mind. I just did what every red-blooded American boy did in those days, the Korean War being in progress. I walked out of that courtroom, into the Navy Recruiting Office across the street, and joined the Navy. This was, without a doubt, one of the smartest things I have ever done.

It took the U.S. Navy about five days to straighten my rebellious ass right out. In fact, it was in boot camp in San Diego that my entire future was shaped. Navy boot camp in those days was eleven weeks of almost total deprivation from anything familiar. For the first seven weeks there was no liberty (a navy euphemism for shore leave and other debauchery) whatsoever. Although this period of total abstinence was probably the best thing that could have happened to my liver, it did little for my disposition. For a guy that could drink the better part of a case of beer in any given sitting, I had managed to generate a powerful thirst. I hit town that Saturday afternoon with only one thing in mind. All I wanted was an ice-cold Pabst Blue Ribbon. Now, San Diego is a great liberty port, but for a teenage sailor wearing the single white stripe of a Seaman Recruit, I might as well have been in Saudi Arabia. In fact, I have been in Saudi Arabia many times since then, and it is infinitely easier to find a beer there that it was for me on that first liberty in seven weeks in San Diego. I returned to the barracks cursing my girlfriend and that cop, cursing the judge in Alabama, and above all, cursing the State of California for their inane drinking laws. As it usually does, fate stepped in.

One of my buddies got back to the barracks about the same time I did, and he obviously had not shared my misfortune of running afoul of the California alcoholic beverage control laws. Once he became mildly coherent again, I asked him where he managed to find the wherewithal to partake of the grape. He shared with me that his cousin, who had entered the Navy several months ahead of him, was undergoing post boot camp training at the Fleet Sonar School, just out the back gate of the Naval Training Center, where we were housed. Of particular significance in this pearl of intelligence was the fact that the Sonar School had an Enlisted Men's Club that was rather lax on checking IDs. After eighteen years of virtually wandering in the wilderness and searching for the burning bush, my life's calling suddenly crystallized. I wanted to go to sonar school and become a *sonarman*.

Coincidentally, our company was scheduled for personnel interviews the following Monday, whereby we could indicate a preference for a navy occupation and formal training, if qualified, and if our desires met the needs of the Navy. In spite of my dismal scholastic record in high school, my Navy aptitude scores were quite high across the board. At my interview, I was adamant that the only reason I had joined the Navy was to become the best sonarman that the Navy had ever produced, like my father and his father before him. The personnelman conducting the interview, obviously not being overly troubled with the smarts himself, didn't see fit to quiz me further, leaving us both totally unfazed by the fact that the science of sonar was then less than ten years old.

In case *you* are wondering not only what sonar is, but also what my point is, I will answer both questions. Sonar is the electronic technique whereby enemy submarines are detected, tracked, and attacked using underwater acoustics. Sonarmen, using highly sophisticated electronic equipment, are the "Ears of the Fleet". They apply this "art", and it is just that, aboard destroyers, minesweepers, aircraft, helicopters, and submarines. The discipline is called Anti-Submarine Warfare (ASW), and it is, still today, a major Navy program. Sonarmen were also required to maintain the equipment, thus an education in electronics was also included in the six-month curricula.

I might not have been the best sonarman the Navy ever produced, but I was up there. I achieved the rank of Sonarman First Class (E-6) during my four-year tour, a rare feat. More significantly, I found a career calling, went to college on the GI Bill, getting a Bachelor's Degree in Electrical Engineering, and spent twenty years working with the Navy in the field of ASW development with Western Electric Company, Bell Telephone Laboratories, Tracor, Inc., of Austin, Texas, and Tracor Marine, Inc., of Port Everglades, Florida, a subsidiary of Tracor. Most important to me, I feel by so doing that I gave something back to the Navy, a debt I can probably never fully repay. I didn't know where I was headed when the Navy took me in, but I sure wasn't bound for the privilege of running for the United States Congress.

There are two other major happenings in my thirty-three year professional business career that I feel perhaps prepared me to at least think I could take on a sitting incumbent for national office. The significance of these two examples will, I trust, become apparent as we get into the political nuances further into these pages.

Certainly, having run for national office is a high point in my life, even though I lost. Such would be a high point in almost anyone's life. However, there are two other accomplishments of which I am quite proud. They both occurred in the early 1980s. They both occurred while I was working for Tracor Marine in Port Everglades, Florida, and both serve to show that I have never been particularly deterred by long odds.

In 1979, I was reassigned from a management role in Tracor Marine's ASW Programs Office into a senior management role in the company's more traditional business of marine engineering. The company had just received a couple of new Navy contracts and several managers were reassigned.

One of the contracts was to provide ocean and inland salvage and harbor clearance operations anywhere in the South Atlantic Ocean, Caribbean Sea, and inland waters entering thereto, on an "as needed" basis. Almost concurrently, our parent company, Tracor, Inc. had been awarded a major subcontract with a Joint Venture prime contractor, HBH (Hughes Aircraft, Bendix Corporation, and Holmes and Narver). This was a Foreign Military Sales (FMS) contract between the U.S. Government and the Kingdom of Saudi Arabia, wherein the United States was to provide thirteen highly sophisticated patrol frigates to Saudi Arabia, train Saudi naval personnel required to man the vessels, and transition the vessels and crews to Saudi Arabia in a completely operational condition. The contract also specified that support facilities for the ships be built and staffed in-Kingdom at Jeddah, on the Red Sea, and Jubail, on the Arabian Gulf. These were elaborate ship repair facilities.

Tracor's role in this program was to provide the maintenance and supply support for the ships and the crews while the ships were temporarily homeported in Little Creek, Virginia for training, to instruct the Saudi crews in the maintenance of the vessels, and to provide ship support engineering functions at the ship repair facilities in-Kingdom. HBH's contract obligations, as the prime contractor, involved an order of magnitude more responsibility, including weapons training, maintenance set-up in-Kingdom, total program documentation, extensive technical staffing in-Kingdom, U.S. Navy liaison, and a host of other services resulting in a $500 million program to HBH. This program was designated as the Saudi Naval Expansion Program (SNEP). The overall program, including the price of the ships, was in the multi-billion dollar range. At stake was not just billions of dollars to U.S. companies, but a military commitment to a very vital ally at a very critical time. There were essentially two elements to all of this; U.S. based and Saudi-based.

My involvement in this program came when the U.S. based element got into big trouble. The ships began arriving at Little Creek, Virginia and the Saudi crews, fresh from training at a host of U.S. Navy technical commands throughout the country converged as well to begin at-sea indoctrination. For reasons that will be established, HBH wasn't equipped to receive the vessels or train the crews, and Tracor wasn't manned and ready to support HBH in maintaining the vessels and getting them ready, or to sustain the vessels in going to sea. The Navy, understandably and rightfully, prepared to bring a judgment of contract default against HBH, Tracor, and perhaps others for non-performance of the contract. This was one of the largest contracts our parent company had ever had, and there was very grave concern at all levels within the company.

Tracor Marine, the subsidiary for which I worked was, first and foremost, a ship repair company and we operated a very successful commercial shipyard in Port Everglades, Florida. Our parent company, Tracor, Inc., was primarily an electronics manufacturing company with little corporate expertise in things nautical. Our president and I were sent to Little Creek to assess the situation and to recommend a course of action to put the program back on track. Arriving there, we found three Saudi ships "hard down" and unable to go to sea. We also found woefully inadequate staffing and a host of other potentially fatal flaws in tooling and equipment. Morale was totally non-existent. A fist fight actually erupted outside the Maintenance Manager's office the first day we were there, while we were meeting with him. He just got up and shut the door, indicating that such was not an isolated occurrence.

Our esteemed president was already in over his head with his own job of trying to manage our shipyard in South Florida, a job for which he was not even remotely qualified. He certainly had no stomach for the situation we found in Little Creek. Furthermore, I think he saw no chance of turning the program around, and he wanted to be as far away as he could when the program cratered. He solved *his* immediate problem easily enough by shoving me into the breach, naming me General Manager, and going home to his slide-rule and his young wife.

The prime contractor, HBH, was in a similar condition. They had recently replaced their top manager with a recently retired Navy Captain, a man named Jim Allingham. Jim had been aboard only a couple of months, and was starting to get a handle on his part of the problem. However, the non-performance of Tracor was about to kill the whole program. What Jim found when he arrived was a huge bureaucracy of retired government employees that had been put in place by his predecessor. What I found was something similar, compounded by the fact that within the bureaucracy that my predecessor had put in place, there were a lot of ex-government shipyard management types, but nobody that knew how to actually repair ships.

The Navy Admiral in charge of the program, and whose back was also against the wall did not mince words. He sat Jim and I down, said he had a letter in his briefcase recommending cancellation of the HBH contract, and said he would give us thirty days to get the program back on track. He also said he would be back in exactly thirty days for a full briefing on our progress, and he expected to see the ships at sea.

Jim and I hit it off immediately and I think we both recognized the problem. We certainly recognized the situation we both were in. My problem was that the management personnel that Tracor had hired had managed to recreate a miniature replica of a Navy shipyard, complete with all the paperwork, approval cycles, layers of management, and other bullshit that makes Navy shipyards models of inefficiency. A surprising amount of this bureaucratic nonsense was actually written into Tracor's contract, along with other restrictions that were totally inconsistent with putting ships to sea.

After a few twenty-hour days of digging through reams of conflicting directives, inane instructions, unworkable concept papers, and several hundred personnel records, I went to Jim and told him that I was going to have to do some things that weren't in the contract, ignore a bunch of things that were, and fire a bunch of people. I also told him that the new staffing was not going to look anything like what was required in our contract. Jim was up to his ass in his own swampload of alligators and gave me carte blanche, including a "license to kill". I literally raided our commercial shipyard in Port Everglades for every skilled worker I could get my hands on for a 30 day "loan" period and immediately put them to work on the three ships that were down. I then began raiding every commercial shipyard in the Tidewater area of Norfolk for skilled marine craftsmen. I fired layers of management and didn't bother to replace them, and totally scrapped the inane repair approval system that had been put in place. For example, every repair request had a ten-person approval cycle to undergo, which, in itself took three or four days to make the rounds of all the various "desks". My rationale was that hardly ever would a repair request be disapproved, so why have an approval cycle. If it's broke, just fix it.

The operation was transformed from a Navy type repair operation to a commercial ship repair operation literally overnight. We had two ships underway in less than two weeks, and the third was up during the third week. In the meantime, we had received two more ships, and they were "up" and being outfitted. We also started force-feeding work into a little marine repair shop I had started for Tracor Marine in the area, and into similar "down river" shops with quick turnaround capability. Rather than trying to draw parts from the Navy Supply System, with 30-45 day lead-times, we literally manufactured the parts in two to three days.

Compounding the problem was the "cold war" that had materialized between the U.S. Navy contingent charged with the overall supervision of the program and the Saudi Navy staff that was paying all the bills for the inefficiency they were observing on a daily basis. First of all, U.S. Navy staffing of a program such as SNEP was outside the normal "career path" of officers pre-selected for greater things to come, meaning that officers ordered to "special project" duty such as this had been generally passed over for promotion and were merely putting in their time waiting to get out or to go to some other dead-end job. They tended to take out their frustrations on the Saudi naval officers.

On the other hand, the Saudi crews, essentially one generation out of the desert and off the backs of camels were understandably intimidated by the state-of-the-art naval technology that confronted them in the form of the sophisticated naval weapons system that had been thrust upon them, and which they were expected to master. They tended to vent their anger and their dislike of the U.S. Navy by taking it out on my workers, who were the most visible because they were working aboard their ships everyday. To the Saudi psyche, uncertainty manifests itself in arrogance. Jim had already broken this code and he explained it to me one night over a bottle of vodka. I had merely assumed that anyone who ran around wearing a Pizza Hut tablecloth and fan belt on their heads and who was raised in a family environment where the daddy wore a dress and the mother wore a sack over her head understandably had a few quirks. His rationale was more psychologically sound, but mine made more sense to me. Nevertheless, understanding this didn't make it any easier and I was still somewhat perplexed as to why the Saudi captains were so cold to me in spite of the fact that the program was dramatically turning around. The reason for this treatment became clear during my third week on site when I was invited, "summoned" is a better word, to have coffee with the senior Saudi ship captain.

Captain Al-Jonas welcomed me tentatively to his wardroom and poured me a half-cup of coffee. He looked me square in the eyes and said, "Ah, Jacobs is a Hebrew name, no"? My problem became crystal clear.

"No, Captain, Jacob is Hebrew. *Jacobs* is redneck. Do you understand redneck, Captain?" I replied.

"Yes, I think I have heard the term. Would you like more coffee?" That solved that problem. I was later told that the Saudis had concerned themselves with little else since I first stepped aboard the waterfront, so concerned were they that a Jew was in charge of repairing their vessels. They had finally nominated Captain Al-Jonas to initiate a confrontation to get to the heart of the matter. Of course, I didn't see any point in burdening them with the fact that my wife was Jewish, a fact that surfaced much later.

The atmosphere on the waterfront cleared over night, and I soon got a chance to solidify my relationship with the Saudis that carried me through the next three years of the program.

Every Friday morning there was a big meeting between the senior Navy brass, the Saudi Commodore, a dozen or so "suits" from Washington, Jim and I, and whoever else might have something to contribute. The stated purpose was to assess the progress of the past week; the actual purpose was a forum for the Navy to beat up on the Saudi Commodore, Captain Al-Fasi, a minor Saudi prince. They had hundreds of princes. The previous afternoon one of the ships returning to the pier after a day of underway training had managed to suck a mooring line into their propellers trying to come alongside the pier in a heavy wind. This is not an everyday occurrence, but it does happen. We had divers in the water within thirty minutes and had the line cut out of the wheel within a couple of hours. No big deal. However, the Navy made it a big deal in the meeting. The Navy commander in charge of the briefing berated the Saudi commodore for a full thirty minutes on the stupidity and lack of seamanship of the Saudi crew. He just wouldn't let up and Captain Al-Fasi, obviously feeling like a piece of dog shit, just had to sit there and take it. Everyone in the room was embarrassed and the Commodore looked like he wished he were back in the desert on his trusty camel. I was sitting across the table from the Commodore and when the tirade finally ended I calmly said, "Commodore, you know that our divers had your mooring line free in only a couple of hours last night. Did you wonder how we were able to free that line so quickly?"

Not at all sure where I was going with this, but looking for any port in the storm, and picking up on anything as a matter of survival, the Commodore answered meekly, "Yes, we did wonder about that."

"Well, I'll tell you how. We've had an awful lot of practice cutting goddamn mooring lines out of the goddamn wheels of goddamn U.S. Navy ships. That's how."

Of course the U.S. Navy commander went totally nonlinear, but I had enough Navy friends. What I needed were a few Saudi friends.

On the twenty-ninth day, the day before the Admiral's visit, I rented a light aircraft, took a camera, and went flying.

The Admiral showed up, as scheduled, with his entourage of thirty or so "experts" from Washington. The meeting convened with Jim Allingham making a few opening remarks, and then he turned it over to me. I got up, lowered the lights, and threw a slide on the projector. It was a shot of an empty pier, taken from the air. I left it up for about 30 seconds, not saying a word, and then put another slide up of another empty pier. This routine went on for about four slides, and I still had not opened my mouth. Everyone in the room was starting to get nervous at what was getting into the third minute of a mute presentation. Finally the Admiral said, "What the hell kind of presentation is this?"

I turned up the lights, took the slide off the projector, and said, "Admiral, your fucking ships are at sea."

He sat there for a brief second, noticeably stunned, then he almost smiled and said, "Very well. Carry on," picked up his briefcase, and left the room, leaving his entire entourage just sitting there looking like deer caught in the headlights.

I think I read the Admiral right that day. Admirals are not accustomed to being answered in quite that manner, hence the stunned expression. However, Admirals don't get to be Admirals by being dumb, and I think he also suddenly realized that we had just solved *his* problem. I never saw him after that day. He was given a promotion and transferred to another job. There was no further talk of a contract default.

Thus, it was pretty much all downhill after the first month or so. The Saudis loved us, the Navy tolerated me, and Allingham covered my ass from his bosses, who were pretty much on a par with the U.S. Navy brass. My maintenance manager and I were invited to Saudi Arabia to welcome the first three ships in-Kingdom. We were the only Americans allowed on the pier when the ships arrived in Jeddah. The Navy was confined behind a barrier at the pierhead.

It was during this visit that the Saudi admiral asked me if I would consider coming to Saudi Arabia as the General Manager of one of the two Saudi ship repair facilities. Flattered though I was, there were a number of reasons why I didn't want the job. "Face" is almost as important to the Saudis as it is to the Japanese. I gave them an out by confiding that my wife was Jewish, knowing this would end *that* discussion. To my utter astonishment, the Admiral summoned me the following day and allowed as how his government would arrange for a visa for my wife if I would accept the position. I'll bet one could count on one hand the permanent visas that have ever been issued to a Jewish woman to live in Saudi Arabia. As graciously as I could, I still declined.

Jim Allingham and I made one hell of a team during the three years we worked that program. His job was an order of magnitude bigger than mine, and he is one of the best large program managers I have ever met. Together, we delivered all thirteen ships to Saudi Arabia under budget and eight months ahead of schedule. I will never forget the day the last five Saudi ships sailed from Little Creek, Virginia for Saudi Arabia. There must have been 300 people standing around on the pier, shaking hands with each other and slapping each other on the back. After three years on this job, neither Jim nor I had ever seen any of them before. They were all from Washington. Jim looked at me and deadpanned as only he can, "Who are all these assholes"?

That job was one of the high points of my career.

Another job of which I am very proud, and which bears on this narrative, occurred during the same period. Thirty large unmanned grain barges slipped their moorings during a flood on the Arkansas River, and careened down the river before thirteen of them struck a dam and sank. The dam, Dam #2 near Dumas Arkansas, was vital in maintaining the navigation pool that permits barge and other navigational water traffic to transit from New Orleans as far inland as Oklahoma. The dam had thirteen spill gates, and the barges wreaked havoc with the dam, jamming some gates in the full "open" position and some in the fully "closed" position. Such a configuration on a gated dam causes severe scouring of the riverbed adjacent to and underneath the dam, and can cause the dam to be undermined, leading to catastrophic failure. The dam was also weakened by the forces of the tons of steel from the wreckage piled up against the dam.

This was the situation the salvage team found when we got to the salvage site in December 1982. Tracor Marine had received a large salvage contract from the Navy that I mentioned earlier, and this was our first major salvage job under this contract.

Allingham had given me a couple of months off from the Saudi contract to head up this salvage effort. The job would be unique because there were thirteen salvage operations to be conducted at one site. It was also unique in that every salvage situation was totally different, requiring a vast repertoire of salvage techniques. It was also a very dangerous job, because the dam could collapse at any given time. Had that occurred, there would certainly have been loss of life, because we were working on, and immediately adjacent to the up-river side of the dam. Millions of dollars in equipment would also have been swept away by the unrelenting forces of the river current.

This book is not about salvage operations, and I will spare the reader the salvage details, other than to say that the Tracor Marine team managed to save the dam and clear the wreckage in 60 days of round-the-clock operations. We also did this job ahead of schedule and under budget. Even more important, we completed the job with no loss of life, or even serious injury. This is phenomenal because, during the first three weeks at the site, the river current was running about eight knots, or about the same as the river current immediately upstream of Niagara Falls. There were tons of debris, both floating and submerged, and our divers were rigging underwater, much of the time with zero visibility. The Salvagemaster for this operation was Leon "Bo'sun" Ryder, a long-time friend, and also a campaign contributor to my run for Congress.

Nor was this job without its lighter moments. One of these involves a lawsuit and the other involves "Buck Knives". When taking on a salvage job, with all the inherent uncertainties, one thing *is* certain; a civil lawsuit will ensue. This is because in order for our company to get involved in a salvage situation under a government contract, the owner of the wreck must have abandoned the wreck. It then falls to the government to remove the wreckage in order to clear the waterway. This is not a free ride for the owner, however, because once the damages have been assessed, the government will look to the owners for restitution. Knowing this, the owners will generally hire a salvage expert of their own to refute the government's claim for damages and to try and prove that the wreck removal could have been accomplished more efficiently than it actually was. All of this is a "given".

In this particular instance, the owners hired a retired salvagemaster that must have been at least 102 years old. For this reason, I wouldn't let him on the dam or aboard the heavy-lift equipment, but instead relegated him to the riverbank, where he could see everything we were doing. I even gave him a copy of our daily salvage report that we generated for the Navy.

Since it doesn't get any colder than Dumas, Arkansas in the winter, he got in the habit of sitting in his car with the heater running to make his observations. Every afternoon after lunch, being warm and comfortable, he would invariably fall asleep. Concurrently, every afternoon after lunch, I would have one of my guys take his picture with one of those cameras that also records the time and date on the print. We must have had twenty-five such shots.

A couple of years later when the civil suit for damages came to trial in a maritime court in New Orleans, this old gentleman spent three days on the stand giving expert testimony of everything we had done "wrong". First of all, the only way to do a salvage job wrong is to either fail to cure the situation, or to make it worse. If you have managed to clear the wreckage, you have done the job "right". When it became our turn, we merely threw up our slides of their "expert" asleep at the switch. After about a dozen such exhibits, the judge put a stop to it and awarded in our favor.

The "Buck Knife Caper" was a little different, because we did enjoy some culpability in this scenario. On this type of job, we bought a lot of "things". In fact we were spending about $50,000 per day. These expenses included salaries, per diem, rental cars, heavy equipment leases, consumables, and a host of other legitimate expenses. Since we were on a government contract, everything had to be approved by a government representative and everything had to be accounted for. We gave a daily list to the Navy of all purchases made and they fell into one of three categories. There were those purchases that were absolutely accountable, such as generators, compressors, and other major items with a useful life exceeding this particular job that would become the property of the government. The second category were items that could be expendable, such as hand tools, foul weather gear, hand-held power tools, wire rope, chain, etc. These would be turned in after the job was over if they were still around and hadn't been lost over the side or broken. The third category were consumables; things that would be used up such as welding rods, oxygen, helium, fuel, etc.

Since all of our workers were "tethered" whenever they were on a wreck, due to the dangerous ambient conditions, I made sure all hands has a reliable Buck knife in case they had to cut themselves loose from a tether. We bought twenty-seven Buck knives at a cost of about $30 each. These fell into the category of equipment that would be returned at the end of the job if they hadn't been lost or whatever.

When the job ended and we were turning in equipment and packing to go home, the head man for the U.S. Army Corps of Engineers, who was the Navy's "customer" on this job, stormed into my office trailer. He was livid and was screaming something about, "Three-piles-of-equipment-ten-feet-high-and-not-one-goddamn-Buck-knife,"   or words to that effect. He demanded that I search everyone's baggage before he would allow anyone off the salvage site. He was almost incoherent.

We had been on this site for 60 days without a day off. We had saved their dam, cleared their wreckage, piled the debris where they wanted it, and restored the river to navigation. We did so 30 days ahead of schedule, and almost a million dollars under budget, and he was worried about 30 Buck knives. I just looked at him and said, "The only Buck knife I know anything about is in my pocket, where it's going to stay. On some jobs, it's Rolex watches, and on some jobs it's Buck knives. You're lucky, yours was a Buck knife job." Of course, he complained to the Navy and I think he even wrote his congressman, but I've still got my Buck knife. To this day, I cannot walk into the Navy Supervisor of Salvage Office in Washington without somebody good-naturedly hard-assing me about those Buck knives. I think they went down in the annals of naval lore along with the strawberries in "The Caine Mutiny" and the palm trees in "Mr. Roberts".

I have chosen to mention both of these career situations, and the anecdotal asides, for two reasons. Career-wise, both jobs looked impossible at first blush. That both jobs were successfully completed instilled some things in me that have made it possible for me to undertake other challenges with a confidence I might not have otherwise been able to bring to bear. From the anecdote side, I think that the end usually justifies the means. Some rules are just meant to be broken. My personal hero is Admiral Hiram Rickover. At his retirement ceremony, the final one, he made the statement, "I have always obeyed all orders...that I agreed with." I would like for that to be the epitaph engraved on my tombstone…if they ever find the body.

Probably the most universal comment that I became used to hearing when friends and family heard that I was running for Congress was, "Have you lost your goddamn mind"?

I don't think I lost my mind. I just think I was hungry for another, different challenge. Well, I was about to get just that!

2

HOW IT ALL GOT STARTED.

I have never considered myself particularly "political". I am a lifelong Republican, "lifelong" being defined as ever since the first time I registered to vote. As near as I can re-construct it, I think I first registered after I got out of the Navy, and while I was still in college. I must have been around 25 years old. In fact, I probably registered as a Republican because I liked Eisenhower, but I also probably registered so that I could vote for Kennedy. You figure that one out.

I didn't even know to which party my parents belonged until I recently checked with an uncle and was told that they were both Democrats. Well, there were a lot of those in Tennessee then, many having since come to their senses. At any rate, party affiliation meant little to me then, and I tended to vote for "the man". Nor did I follow much in the way of politics. Oh, I followed Kennedy, especially during the Cuban Missile Crisis, because I was involved in that. I went into Guantanamo on one of the aircraft sent to evacuate the military dependents. I was a tech rep for Western Electric Company and I was sent down to install some electronic equipment to support the blockade.

I also followed Johnson closely, because I was living in Japan at the time, and I was in and out of Vietnam and throughout the Far East, collecting acoustic intelligence for the Navy. Watergate kept my interest, as it did that of many people because we were living in Washington at the time, but I was never really interested much below the Presidential level. If pressed, I could probably have named one of my two senators but I doubt if I would have known the name of my congressman.

Probably the most influential person in my political "education" was Jim Allingham, with whom I worked closely on the Saudi program, for whom I served as best man at his fourth and, I'm sure, his final wedding, and with whom I try to stay in touch. This is growing exceedingly difficult since he and his wife, Liz purchased a 37-foot mobile home and a Bronco and "hit the road". I've even got a feeling politics had something to do with that, so disgusted as he had become with the outcome of the 1996 General Election wherein Clinton retained his presidency.

Jim was the type of political observer who used to yell at the TV, and he referred to the McLaughlin Group TV show as the "Saturday Night Fights". I spent a lot of time with the Allinghams for a number of years because they lived in Washington and I was spending a lot of time there with my job. Their home was my home-away-from-home, and even when they moved down to Madison County, Virginia, I spent many weekends with them. Jim was considerably right of me. Hell, Jim was right of Pat Buchanan, but he had the most acute grasp of politics of anyone I have ever known. Nevertheless, the gulf to my right was enough to get us into spirited political arguments, especially if a bottle of vodka was involved, which was usually the case. Certainly, it was during this period in the mid and late 1980s that I began to really appreciate the difference between Republicans and Democrats. Probably the only thing that Jim hated more than Democrats was the Washington Post.

On most weekends when I was at the farm in Madison County, my usual custom on Sunday mornings was to take his Dodge Ram pick-up and drive two or three miles to the 7-11 and get donuts and a Washington Post. I don't think I have ever seen Jim buy a Washington Post in all the years I have known him. I would be sitting on the porch reading it when Jim would finally make it down for coffee. Our Sunday morning ritual never varied. Jim would say, "Well, what's the commie rag sheet have to say today?"

My reply was always the same. "I dunno, Jim, I'm just reading the sports page."

It is also difficult to spend a lot of time in the Washington area without becoming attuned to politics. Absolutely *everything* in that town revolves around the subject. Their local news on TV is, basically, the national news in the rest of the country. In that town, if didn't happen inside the Beltway, it might as well not have happened. It would not have surprised me to see the Oklahoma City bombing reported as, "Federal Building Blown Up Outside the Beltway".

Probably the single event that drew me personally into the political arena was the 1994 Election. I was on an extended stay in Washington on business, and I was living in our condo in Crystal City. Most of my socializing was with people living in Crystal City. This is a bustling governmental center by day, with most of the Navy procurement and engineering commands being housed there. But after dark, as the last commuter train leaves and the last Happy Hour reveler stumbles off to the suburbs to mother and the kids, it becomes a surprisingly tight social group comprised of the residents living there. In fact, a number of members of congress lived in our building and the building next to ours. As the election drew near, and as the bar talk shifted to politics, it became shockingly apparent that most of my newfound friends were Democrats. This disturbing bit of trivia had never come up before. Even more appalling was the fact that these "acquaintances" were dead-set against Ollie North in his bid for the Senate seat from Virginia.

Now, I've got to tell you, Ollie North is one of my heroes. Furthermore, in the whole Iran-Contra affair, I have never been completely convinced that a crime was even committed. Selling arms to the Iranians at an inflated price, paying the government for the cost of the arms, and applying the profit to a cause that is in the interest of the United States, with *nothing* going into the pockets of elected government officials or Oliver North, or his "partners", other than a modest fee for their involvement is, in my opinion, ingenious. Where I grew up, it is also called "free enterprise". It was a great plan. The fact that North lied to Congress, for which he was charged, and for which he was convicted, was a miscarriage of justice. First of all, when one such as North is in a position to conduct clandestine operations for our military, and is sworn to absolute secrecy, sharing this information with the Congress is about as irresponsible as sharing it with the Washington Post. The result will be the same. Putting it another way, lying to Congress seems to pale when one considers that they lie to you every day. Had I been elected, I might feel a little differently about this, but not much. In my opinion, Congress has a long way to go before they earn the complete trust of this taxpayer.

At any rate, that was my feeling at the time, and I agreed to host an election party at my condo. Since it was my party, the theme was, "Go Get'Em, Ollie". I even lifted a dozen or so "North for Congress" signs on the day of the election with which to paper the walls in decoration (forgive me, Ollie, I didn't know what it meant until my campaign to have your signs stolen).

Of course, North lost his bid for a Senate seat, and I sometimes wonder if the Democrats wouldn't rather have him in their midst as a junior Republican Senator rather than with his own nationally syndicated radio talk show. Sometimes, it's better to have someone inside the tent pissing out, than outside the tent pissing in. But the big news was that the Republicans had won the Congress.

I will swear to you, that possibility, nor the ramifications thereof, never even crossed my mind until the following days. In fact, I did not realize that the Democrats had held control of the Congress for the past forty years. When this fact sunk in, it took a little while for me to even understand what that really meant. I did not realize that for over forty years no Republican had ever chaired a committee. I did not realize that for over forty years a Republican bill, no matter how worthy, probably had never made it to the floor for a vote. I did not realize that for over forty years the Republican Members of Congress had been little more than galley slaves aboard the Ship-of-State. I guess I really did not realize that the $4.5 trillion dollar national debt, the fact that the Medicare program was facing bankruptcy, the fact that billions of dollars had been stolen from the Social Security Trust Fund, the fact that American taxpayers were paying half their income in direct and indirect taxes to feed the federal bureaucracy, and the fact that the result was that the national economy was a house of cards that could collapse at any minute, could all be laid at the feet of the Democratic leadership.

I am an engineer. Engineers don't operate on knee-jerk reaction. We are trained to think logically. We are sometimes slow to get there, but we get there. Once I got there, I got suitably pissed. Allingham was not an engineer, and he had figured this out long before I did, which I guess explains why he got pissed before I did.

The bright spot in all of this was that seventy-six new Republican Congressmen came to Congress. Not one Republican running for re-election had lost his/or her seat in that election. They came in on the most exciting mandate in history, promising to enact the "Contract With America", a ten-point "start" to turn the country around. The new Republican Congress promised to pass this legislation through the House in the first one hundred days, and they passed nine of them. The one that failed to pass was Term Limits.

Even more meaningful to me personally, and what triggered something inside me, was the fact that well over half of these new Members, who would become known as the infamous "Freshman Class", had no prior political experience and were, for the most part, *businessmen*. For me to have time on my hands *and* be thinking at the same time is a pretty dangerous combination.

At the time, I had our condo on the market and I wrote a letter to all of the incoming freshmen and I included a brochure on the condo, hoping to sell it to one of them. During the Special Session in December, when they were all in town for orientation, several of the new Members and their wives came to inspect the property. This gave me a chance to speak first hand with them and learn about their motivation for making such a sacrifice as putting themselves through a grueling campaign. I was amazed to learn that they felt exactly as I did about the sorry state wherein the country had been placed by the unbridled spending on scores of failed social programs and other massive wastes of taxpayer money by the Democratic leadership. To a man, they felt they could do something about it. The idea that I was certainly as qualified to do that job as were these new Members, with whom I was talking, began to crystallize in my mind.

The opening weeks of the 104th Congress were really an exciting time to be in Washington. The new Republican Congress passed numerous bills on the *first day*, which went a long way toward starting to reform Congress and to make the Congress accountable and subject to the same laws that everyone else must obey. It was during this period that Newt Gingrich rose to power and, in so doing, embraced the freshman class. I am well aware that, for a while, Gingrich was one of the most unpopular men in this country. Boy, am I ever aware of that fact. However, you must realize that for over forty years, Republican House Members had been sitting on the back-bench with little or no power to get anything done. And now, overnight, the Republican Party had been transformed into the party in power. For the first time in over forty years the Republicans were the ones that cracked the whip over the *new* galley slaves.

It is really no wonder, given this heady atmosphere that the House Freshmen, and their leader, Gingrich, ran into trouble. First of all, I do not deny that there was considerable arrogance coming from the right side of the aisle. But considering what had just transpired, I can certainly understand *why* it happened. Furthermore, I still think Newt Gingrich had flashes of great brilliance, which have since been diminished with his handling of his ethics problem. I think his "Contract With America" was exactly what we needed at the time, and we still need it because, although nine of the ten items passed the House in the first one hundred days, exactly as promised, few of these items have actually become law. However, the reality is that Gingrich came across to the public as an arrogant asshole and the freshmen came across as his willing spear-chuckers. I think it was a bum rap, but the Democrats, still smarting from their crushing defeat during the 1994 election, drew their wagons in a circle and did a masterful job of fanning the flames with a steady barrage of lies and more lies.

A lot of this is in retrospect. During the spring of 1995 though, watching all of these things happening from a front-row seat, I was really becoming interested in getting myself involved in this "revolution". Our condo was just across the Potomac River from Washington, on the fourteenth floor of the Waterford House in Crystal City. It has a commanding view of the Washington skyline, with the Capitol Building showcased in the center of the magnificent panoramic view. When Congress is in session, a white light burns on the Capitol Dome, clearly visible from the master bedroom of our condo. During this time, that light almost never went out before 10 PM and many nights it was still burning after midnight. On more than one occasion, I fell asleep looking at that light. There was clearly a revolution taking place, a long overdue revolution, and I found myself wanting to become a part of it.

Accordingly, during a chance conversation with a friend of mine, who was the property manager of the condominium next door, she told me that the "head of the Florida Republican Party" had an apartment in her building. As it turned out, he was not the party head in Florida, but he was the Republican State Committeeman from Broward County. She knew him and put me in touch with him. His name is David Eller. I called him and told him that I was thinking about becoming a candidate in the coming election. He was very cordial and invited me to come in and talk with him the next time I was in South Florida. Fortunately, I had the good sense to tell him that I had no political background, because that would become quite obvious in the months ahead.

I returned home to South Florida in March 1995 and contacted Barbara Collier, the Vice-Chairman of the Broward Republican Executive Committee (BREC). She was very encouraging and readily agreed to see me and, just on the basis that I was *thinking about running for Congress,* invited me down that afternoon to meet Lamar Alexander, who was in town as part of his campaign for President. I vaguely knew who he was, but I had another commitment, and declined. This was the first instance, although I did not recognize it as such at the time that I saw that even being a candidate for national office does tend to lend itself to access. A meeting with Barbara was scheduled, and this first step even got screwed up. I got lost trying to find the Broward Republican headquarters. This could have been an omen.

Barbara was very supportive, said they were looking for someone with a business background with no political baggage, and said, "You don't happen to be a veteran, do you?" I replied in the affirmative. She seemed very pleased with that answer. Then she asked me about my stand on abortion. I said that I hadn't given it a lot of thought, but that I was probably pro-choice. Wrong answer, she said in so many words, but I blew it off, because, to me, this was a non-issue. I won't say that my initial response was wrong, but it sure wasn't a "non-issue", as I was to find out.

I left her office fairly encouraged. At least they hadn't thrown me out. Quite the contrary; Barbara suggested that I meet with Clay Shaw, the only sitting Republican Congressman from Broward County. Since I was returning to Washington in a few days, she suggested that she set up a meeting for me in Washington.

I already knew Congressman Shaw and I liked him. I had been in business in Broward County since 1975, working on government contracts. In the course of such actions, there are times when one needs the help of one's congressman. A minor problem was that Shaw was not *my* congressman. However, the part of the company that I commanded was in Port Everglades, and the Port *was* in his district.

The first time I met him was when my company won a rather large contract with the U.S. Customs Service to provide maintenance on their rather large fleet of drug interdiction vessels in the Southeast Region of the United States. It is not necessarily customary, but it makes good business sense to inform one's congressman when one does something to increase the job base in that congressional district. They like that stuff. The meeting was essentially a "wash" because the company I had previously worked for, Tracor Marine, had shut down a shipyard in the Port, which cost about the same amount of jobs that I had just won. He made a point of mentioning this to me. I explained that I was not a corporate officer in *that* company, but that I was a corporate officer in *this* company, and I think we parted as friends.

I might add that I attempted to extend the same courtesy to Larry Smith, the Democratic Congressman, who *was* my Congressional Representative at the time, but I was unable to get an appointment. However, I was on a flight from Washington to Ft. Lauderdale a few weeks later and Smith and I were both seated up front on an Eastern Airlines flight. Not only did I live in Smith's district, the same district for which I have just run, but my company's main office was also in his district. I introduced myself to Smith, and attempted to tell him of the good fortune that had just befallen us both with the Customs contract. His reception could not possibly have been more aloof. There was no mistaking his attitude that I was *bothering him.* At that time, I said to myself, *"That man is an asshole!"*

In the ensuing months, I had a lot of fun at Larry's expense in the Letters to the Editor section of the Ft. Lauderdale Sun- Sentinel. At one point, when Smith was named as a leading proponent of using the Senate banking facility as a source of interest-free personal loans to cover his ineptness in the pursuit of games of chance and other debauchery, real or imagined, I was asked by a Sun-Sentinel reporter if I had ever considered running for his seat. "No Way," I recoiled, "I have a *real job.* " Well, things change, but it's interesting to look back on what got you to do what you did. Our EX-CONgressman definitely played a role in my decision. I should have done it sooner.

The next contact I had with Clay Shaw was in the aftermath of Hurricane Hugo, which devastated the U.S. Virgin Islands. My company had two major contracts with the Navy that entailed facilities on the island of St. Croix. We had approximately fifty employees there, plus a couple of company-owned ships, and we were responsible for a Navy testing facility worth several million dollars. Hurricane Hugo essentially leveled the island, along with the government facility. It also wiped out the homes of *all* of our employees, as well as all communication facilities back to the mainland. The Pentagon had managed to mobilize local National Guard Forces on the island in the aftermath of the storm, and these very same forces became the major pillagers and looters in St. Croix, a fact never widely reported.

It was a couple of days before we were able to establish radio contact with one of our ships in St. Croix. The Captain reported that all of our employees, who had lost everything, had made their way to our ship, which had just been replenished with food for an impending navy mission. The ship, along with all of our employees and their dependents, totaling over one hundred and fifty people, was forced to "stand out" from the pier to keep from being boarded by looters led by the Virgin Islands National Guard.

After this phone patch reached me through the overseas marine operator, I immediately contacted Clay Shaw's office. His aide connected me on a conference call to some high ranking civilian at the Pentagon, who, after some persuading, agreed to recommend that President Bush send federal troops into St. Croix, rather than more local National Guard, who were the major cause of the problem.

The point is, although I had briefly met him, Shaw only knew that I was a quasi-constituent, whose employees needed immediate help. He trusted the "voice on the phone", took action, and averted a major crisis. I made it a point to schedule a meeting with Congressman Shaw on a subsequent trip to Washington to de-brief him on the outcome of his intervention, which resulted a totally positive outcome. His reaction to this de-briefing was one of appreciation, making the comment to the effect that it was rare that he ever received any feedback on the outcome of his actions on the behalf of a constituent.

Before heading back to Washington, I also had lunch with David Eller, the Broward County State Committeeman. David is probably one of the top fund-raisers in South Florida, and I knew that. In retrospect, I think he was pretty much underwhelmed by my grasp of what I was talking about doing. I am also sure that my lack of political savvy came shining through, because I really hadn't thought much of this through at the time. His parting remark was to the effect that I should plan a "grassroots campaign". This is politi-speak for "you're not going to be able to raise much money, and I'm not going to raise any for you." I didn't, and neither did he.

True to her word, Barbara did contact Congressman Shaw's office and there was a message on my machine when I arrived back in Washington. I did meet with him and his Chief-of-Staff, informed him of my thoughts, and he, too, was generally supportive. Of course, his primary message was that it would take a lot of money to mount an effective campaign. I had heard that before, of course, but at the time I merely blew it off because I didn't really see any problem in attracting the necessary funding. Little did I know how difficult this would come to be.

During this meeting, Shaw also made a curious statement. He said that he would support me "as much as he could" but went on to add that the Florida Congressional Delegation had an agreement among themselves not to campaign against each other during elections. At the time I thought this was rather odd, and I still think that way. As in all questions, there are two sides. On the one hand, South Florida, which is made up of Monroe, Dade, Broward, and Palm Beach Counties, has eight congressional seats, evenly divided between Republicans and Democrats. This sub-delegation usually votes together on what is good for South Florida. This is the upside and is as it should be. The downside is how this alliance effects Florida, as a whole, and to some extent, Congress as a whole. Control of the House is critical, now more than ever before if this country is going to survive. *Congressional seats are damned important commodities!* Millions of dollars are spent on many congressional campaigns with many big dollars legally coming from both the national committees. So what's this "gentlemen's agreement" bullshit?

I look at this as I have always looked at wagering on the game of golf. As you who play the game know, in any given foursome there is usually a team bet, and then each player usually has an individual bet with the other members of the foursome. On about the last three holes, when all bets have probably been doubled, and with more money riding on the individual bets because there are more of them, my approach to this situation has always been *screw the team. It's every man for himself.*

In politics, as in golf, I feel that as long as you play by the rules, you can beat the hell out of your opponent and still remain friends. My understanding is that several state delegations have such a non-compete "hand-shake", but it is also my understanding that such agreements are frowned upon by the national committees of both parties. I think they should be. Had I been elected, I would not have signed up for this alliance.

One of the most encouraging calls I made while in Washington was to Senator Connie Mack, our Republican Senator. It was here that I was beginning to realize that being even an unannounced candidate gets one a certain amount of access. A meeting was easily scheduled and Senator Mack spent about forty-five minutes with me. I probably had my act together a little better by the time this meeting took place. My feeling was that the Senator took me fairly seriously. Of course, he dwelt on the money aspect, but he also threw out a couple of policy questions, which I fielded easily, because I was up on what was going on in Congress at the time, and I was aware of his role in trying to save the Medicare program. Perhaps the best advice he gave me was that if I didn't do anything else, I should be sure to attend "candidate school". Yes, there is such a thing, and it *was* sage advice. I left his office with a strong liking for the man.

This impression was borne out perhaps a year later, after I was an announced candidate, when my wife, Sandy, and I were invited to attend a "meet and greet" in Senator Mack's honor at a major Republican supporter's home on the Intercoastal Waterway in Ft. Lauderdale. We had parked down the street from the house and were walking up to the door just as the Senator arrived in the circular driveway with his driver. He fairly leaped out of the car and approached us, shaking my hand, and inquiring about how the campaign was going. The three of us stood there and chatted for perhaps five minutes. Anyone observing this scene would have thought we had been close friends for years. When we made a move toward the house, Senator Mack insisted we enter with him. Talk about a real class act.

Barbara Collier also put me in touch with the State Republican officials in Tallahassee. David Johnson, the Congressional Liaison Representative, called me and we chatted, mostly about my background. I found it very easy to talk with David. He in turn arranged for Ann McCord, the Director of Field Operations for the Republican National Congressional Committee (NRCC) in Washington, to call me. Since I was in Washington at that time, we arranged a meeting in her office at the NRCC headquarters on Capitol Hill.

Ann is a surprisingly young, no-nonsense woman whose job I can best describe as being den-mother to several hundred congressional hopefuls during every election cycle. I assume her first cut is to subtly discourage anyone she feels might be an unsuitable candidate early in the process. I was still pretty naive, but I knew the demographics that I was facing, and I knew something about the opponent that I would be running against, Peter Deutsch, a second term congressman, with ten years in the Florida State Legislature before that. I don't think that I ever talked with anyone who knew Peter where the terms "arrogant" and "ruthless" did not come up. I also knew he was one of the top fund-raisers in Congress, in spite of his relatively junior status, and his lackluster legislative career to date.

One of the first things out of Ann's mouth was, "You got any skeletons?"

My answer was to the effect that, sure, I had skeletons, doesn't everybody? But there were none that I couldn't handle and I certainly didn't have a skeleton farm. I also made the point that one doesn't carry a Secret or Top Secret security clearance around for over thirty years if they have strayed too far off the straight and narrow. This seemed to satisfy that criteria and that's the last time the subject ever came up. She also made the observation that Deutsch was no angel, either. I don't know what, if anything, she meant by that and I never pursued it.

I guess I passed muster because she took my local address and said she would send out a "Candidate Pack", with some things for me to fill out and return to her. A few days later, a thick manila envelope arrived addressed to me as:

Jim Jacobs
Jim Jacobs for Congress

It had a nice ring.

3

TESTING THE WATERS

Believe it or not "Testing the Waters" is a legal definition coined by the Federal Election Commission (FEC) that allows you to open a campaign account, solicit money, and even spend money without having to declare a candidacy or to file fiscal reports with the FEC. Of course, this is not an open ended status, because once you have either raised $5000, or spent $5000, whichever occurs first, your status changes to "candidate", making it necessary that you declare the candidacy and begin filing stringent reports. The $5000 limit also includes any money of your own that you might put into the account, or lend to the account.

I opened such an account and lent my campaign $1000, just for "walking around money". I was far from making any decision, but since nobody had slammed a door in my face, or otherwise shut me down, I decided to at least see the next card.

The next card was the quarterly meeting of the Florida Executive Committee in Orlando in the summer of 1995. I particularly remember the weekend because the Ryder Cup was being played and for some reason, as yet unexplained, the Hyatt, where we stayed, did not have the event on their cable service. I remember thinking that maybe this excursion into the wonderful world of national politics might bring with it too high a price to pay. Man, I didn't have a clue!

Actually, I attended this meeting at the behest of Barbara Collier specifically to meet with David Johnson and Randy Enright, the Executive Director of the State Republican Party. I have this penchant for wanting to put faces with names, and these names had been coming up a lot. I also wanted to meet Tom Slade, the Chairman of the State Republican Party, to see if I could wrangle an appointment as a Delegate to the Florida Presidential Straw Poll, Presidency III, to be held in Orlando in November. This is Florida's equivalent of a pre-primary, non-binding election wherein the state gets to get a good look at the potential presidential candidates.

Delegates to this convention are determined primarily by lottery, with 85% of the 5000 plus delegates being chosen by lot. The other 15% are appointed by the Chairman and are pretty much reserved for major contributors, party officials, dedicated activists, and other criteria probably known only to the Chairman. State and national candidates usually have a shot at achieving delegate status by this route. I had been unable to participate in the lottery because I was still being kept in Washington on business, and physical presence was required. Barbara had submitted my name on the list of appointees from Broward County, but it had not made the cut.

The meeting with Johnson and Enright went well, I felt, and I was able to buttonhole Tom Slade at one of the hospitality suites during the evening. I stated my case and he said that he had not been aware that I was a candidate. He agreed to take care of it, which he did. My credentials arrived shortly in the mail.

I also think it was about this time that I first contacted Beverly Kennedy. Bev had run against Peter Deutsch twice, in 1992 when the seat was open, and again in 1994. In 1994 she got 39% of the vote. I had never met Bev. In fact, I had never even seen Bev, so little time was I spending in Ft. Lauderdale during those years. When I called her and introduced myself she said, "I was wondering when you were going to call me."

We hit it off pretty well on the phone. She assured me that she had had enough of Deutsch, and definitely would not run again in the 20th District. She was undecided beyond that. She was considering a run in the 19th District, immediately to the north, or, she said, she might do some political consulting for one of the candidates. This interested me at the time, because I had not then relegated political consultants to the realm of luxuries I could not afford. It also occurred to me that, even though Deutsch had beat her, and he might beat me, I couldn't help but wonder if he could beat us both.

I said as much, and I asked her to tell me a little about herself. She answered with, "I'm a damn good-looking 50-year-old, and I've got great legs." Well, hell, being a leg man of some renown, that's reason enough to schedule a face-to-face meeting.

We agreed to meet at the Broward Republican Headquarters in a couple of weeks when I would be back in South Florida. Now, I've got to say that Bev Kennedy can dominate a room, whether there are 200 people present, or three. There were three at this meeting; the two of us, and Barbara Collier.

Bev immediately took charge and after about twenty minutes declared, "You know, we would make a good team. You're all laid back, and I'm right out there."

To which I was able to get in my first words, "Bev, I'm not laid back. You haven't stopped running your mouth since you walked in."

Nevertheless, we became friends and continue to be so. She decided to run for the open seat in District 19, which is probably why we are still friends. Had we teamed up, we would undoubtedly have killed each other. First of all, she's a born again Christian, and I'm not quite there yet.

Presidency III was held early in November 1995 and it was our first taste of big-time politics. Hell, it was our first taste of politics, period. I didn't get back from Washington until two days before the event and there must have been over a hundred pieces of mail, plus about thirty or forty Federal Express (FedEx) packages waiting for me. In the two days before we went to Orlando, we would get two or three FedExes a day from some of the candidates. They did a real full court press on the uncommitted delegates, of which I was one of the few. The vast majority of the Broward delegates were committed to Bob Dole. I was truly undecided, but I was leaning toward Lamar Alexander.

We received a semi-private audience with Governor Alexander in his suite during the event, and I became convinced after listening to him during the debate, and especially after meeting with him personally, that he was the *only* candidate that could beat Clinton. I remain convinced until this day that had a very few things gone just a little bit differently during the primaries, we would have a new president in the White House today.

Here is another man with a lot of class. We had only met with him briefly earlier in the day, and as Sandy and I emerged from the elevator on our way to dinner, we ran right into a crowd of about fifty people clustered around him. Seeing us, he turned to his wife, Honey, and said, "Hey, here's Jim and Sandy".

I wonder how many people he had met that day. I hope he hangs in there and runs in 2000, because I sure don't see anyone else coming down the pike.

It was also at Presidency III that I had my first brief encounter with the press. Steve Bosquet, the very able political columnist for the Miami Herald, came up to me and said that someone had told him that I was running for Congress. I confirmed that I was thinking about it, gave him my card, and that was about it. The following weekend in his column, I received my first press as he reported that, "Jim Jacobs, a ruddy faced gentleman, was passing out cards at Presidency III, saying he was going to challenge Peter Deutsch in the 20th District."

Come on, Steve, you could at least have said "ruggedly handsome". Besides, that's not "rudd", that's scar tissue.

The NRCC Candidate School was scheduled for three days in Washington at the Crystal City Sheraton Hotel almost immediately following Presidency III, so Sandy and I flew back to Washington to attend. Actually, I almost missed it. I made airline reservations for Sandy well in advance, made a "hole" in my work schedule, and did all the things I was supposed to do *except* send in my application for the school. I completely forgot it until about a month before the school when I received notice that applications were closed, and the class was full. I went over to see Ann McCord and managed to bleed on her desk sufficiently that she got me in. I told you she was a den mother.

The NRCC does a lot of things well, and the candidate school was one of these things. It consists of three days of total immersion into the campaign process. Every single thing one needs to know is covered, and it goes from 7:30 in the morning until around ten every night. There are prominent speakers, including quite a few Members, and even sessions where the Members go one-on-one with the candidates. There are special classes for the spouses, with equally impressive speakers. Mrs. Mack and Mrs. Gingrich spoke at a couple of the spouse's sessions. There are TV training classes, sessions on how to handle the press, and numerous sessions on fundraising. On the last night there is a reception for the candidates where we were turned loose on forty or fifty Political Action Committee (PAC) representatives to try out our new "skills". Talk about a three-ring circus. These people have heard every line in the book and we were all running around like a bunch of idiots trying to con them out of a campaign contribution employing our just-learned-today political expertise.

I had an interesting exchange with one young lady, whose PAC will remain anonymous. Most of these representatives are females, by the way, and most of them are quite young. But then to me, I guess everybody is young. This rep asked me who my opponent was and I told her I was running against Peter Deutsch. Without batting an eye she said, "Here's my card. Be in my office in the morning and I'll write you a check."

I didn't take her up on it, however, because I still was far from sure that I was going to do this thing. However, a couple of revelations were starting to sink in; my potential opponent wasn't as revered in the big city as he is in the condos of South Florida, and PACs are a business in the true sense of the word.

One of the high points of the candidate school was a trip to the Capitol for a tour and to meet with Speaker Gingrich. I had been up there many times on business with my company, but I had never had a guided tour and I had never met the Speaker. This excursion had all the trappings of a high school field trip, although I don't know how I should know since I was usually shooting nine-ball when my class went on a field trip.

We all had individual pictures taken with Gingrich and, I'll swear, they ran all 70 candidate couples through the photo-op in twenty minutes. He then spoke with us, outlining his plans for the remainder of the 104th Congress. He said one thing that burned in my brain, but I guess I was too politically non-astute to heed it. Things were starting to get very tense with the Democrats and, of course, the media was putting their usual liberal spin on everything. Gingrich had not started his slide, but he probably foresaw it coming. He told us not to try to defend him or the freshman class when we got on the campaign trail, but just to run our race and stay on message. Well, I stayed on message pretty well, but I did try to defend him and the 104th Congress and I got bloody doing so.

I also fell in love during the school. Well, not really, because the lady is already married and, come to think of it, so am I. Susan Molinari, the Congresswoman from New York's Seventh District gave an impromptu speech at one of our luncheons. I say "impromptu", because her husband, Bill Paxon, the charismatic and very able NRCC Chairman was scheduled and couldn't make it. She is a dynamite speaker with an absolutely effervescent personality. Following her very upbeat remarks, she took a few questions. I raised my hand and was acknowledged. "Will you come to South Florida and campaign for me," I asked.

"Sure," she said. "As long as it is in January or February." We're going to have to move the elections from the Fall to the Spring.

Bob Dole did well to tap her for his Keynote Speaker at the 1996 Republican National Convention. Even though she has left Congress to pursue a career in television, my read on it is that she is merely seeking national name recognition and plans a return to politics within a very few years. In fact, I predict that she will be elected in 2008 as the first female President of the United States when Lamar Alexander retires. Remember, you heard it here.

Several good friends were made during the candidate school and some of them won their elections and got in. It was also interesting to note that over half the class were businessmen, and many of these potential candidates had no prior political experience. Two such candidates come to mind; John Cooksey, a physician from Louisiana made it in and Rose Birtly, a Continental Air Lines executive from New York City did not.

We went away with enough reading material to start a political library and a head full of things we probably wouldn't remember, but all of which would be encountered at one point or another during the campaign. Senator Mack was absolutely right. If anyone who reads this plans to run for Congress, *don't miss this school!*

One of the training aids we came away with was a list of "50 Questions You Had Better Be Able To Answer". These questions are questions about the candidate, the candidacy, and the issues. Many are questions you will be asked, such as "Why Are You Running For Congress". If I heard that once, I heard it a thousand times. I also remember Ted Kennedy being asked that about his bid for the presidency on national TV a few years ago and he fell all over it. It hurt him badly.

More than anything I did while I was "testing the waters", sitting down over the course of several days and putting these answers on paper was probably the most important. First of all, this drill made me look at myself, it made me analyze my strengths and weaknesses, and it made me look at myself the way a voter would look at me. It also brought into focus the enormity of what I was about to undertake, and about how I was going to be able to get from announcing the candidacy through to election day. The questions on the issues were especially revealing. Before I began putting my thoughts into written words, if anyone had asked me I would have said that I was a right-wing conservative. Discussions at the water cooler or in a bar somewhere are one thing. But when you start formulating answers that you are going to have to defend, and which will be going out on TV, and even more important, if you get elected you might have to enact into law, you tend to move a little more toward the middle. I don't want to give the impression that I was formulating these answers just to see what sounded good. I knew that I had to truly *believe* these answers because I was going to be answering these questions in the heat of battle, before live and TV audiences, and before the press, who like nothing better than to catch a candidate in a flip-flop. When one starts putting all these criteria on an answer to a question, one starts thinking through the question very seriously. One also makes sure that what he says is what he truly believes.

I have included these fifty questions and answers in the Appendix. This is not the first draft of that document, but it is the original finished product. I have not gone back and edited it for this book, and I used the document many times in preparing for a debate. I might have softened my answers on the campaign trail to target a particular audience, but I never changed my position on a single issue, and I never got caught in a flip-flop because I did not flip-flop. Moreover, right or wrong, these answers are what I *believe,* and I ran on what I believed.

Probably the single biggest issue in my campaign was abortion. All the polls tell you that the biggest issues were the balanced budget, Medicare, and Social Security. These issues were all up there, but the biggest issue, without a doubt, was *abortion.*

Nor did I have a hard time formulating my answer on this issue. I am pro-choice, and to me that is the common-sense answer. That is the only thing for which I can commend the Democrats. They figured this out, and they are not particularly known for their common sense. Even a blind squirrel picks up an acorn every now and then.

Nor was this going to be an issue between Deutsch and me because he was also pro-choice, and *believe me,* I was looking for issues between us. This just didn't happen to be one of them.

What really seems to escape the Pro-Life bloc is that being Pro-Choice doesn't necessarily mean that you believe that abortion is the right thing to do. It simply means, at least it means to me, that this is really a moral choice and that the individual should have the right to make the choice. It follows that the individual must find it within his or her own conscience to live with that decision. As can be seen from my brief treatment on the subject in the Appendix, I even came up with the idea that if abortion was truly a political issue, perhaps we should put the question to a national referendum. And, *let's not give the men a vote* and see where the issue comes down. My wife nixed the idea, and I did not use this line in answering questions from panelists or from an audience. The only exception came very near the end of the campaign while being questioned on the subject by a very obstreperous man. I threw the line out, pretty much in exasperation, and got another one of those rare spontaneous bursts of applause from the females in the audience. Perhaps I should have used the line all along.

However, in retrospect, I don't think there is a "right" answer on the subject. I ran a very open campaign and my home phone number was right out there, and I received a lot of calls. My E-mail address was also widely published, especially on my Web-Site and on my issue card hand-outs. Most traffic on both mediums involved the abortion issue.

One man called me and identified himself as a Republican Committeeman (precinct captain). He told me that he could not vote for me because I was Pro-Choice. I pointed out that I was against the partial birth procedure, and would have voted to override Clinton's veto of the bill making the procedure illegal, as put forth by the House. I also pointed out that Deutsch had voted not to override the veto, leaving it legal to perform infanticide on babies three minutes away from live birth. I went on to say that I did not support the government paying for abortions, while Deutsch felt that it was a wonderful idea. All of this put me considerably "right" of Deutsch on the issue. No, he still couldn't vote for me because I was advocating "murdering babies".

I asked him the obvious question, "Well, if you can't vote for me, who are you going to vote for?"

His answer: "I'm not going to vote."

Wow! Here is a man who was elected by Republicans to work to get Republican candidates elected in an election in which the entire future of this country is hinging, *and this asshole is not even going to vote!*

In a world where hundreds of thousands of people have died fighting for the right to vote, and where, even this year, people in other parts of the world have stood in line for *days* just to cast a free ballot, he's not going to vote because he disagrees with the Supreme Court of the United States. Well, it is his right, and I served in the military to preserve that right. But, I still don't think he should be a precinct captain.

Another service provided to candidates that is very helpful is provided by GOPAC. This is a candidate education entity that has several facets, including the one that got Gingrich in the trouble he was in. However, the service to which I availed myself was the Wednesday night conference calls. If one is a registered candidate, he or she can dial into a live conference call at 10 PM (EST) and be briefed on, and ask questions about, a Topic of the Week. This Wednesday night event is generally hosted by Rep. John Shadegg (R-AZ), and always has another Member present, who is cognizant on the topic at hand, and who briefs the phone audience and then takes questions. It is also extremely handy for "name dropping".

For instance, in one candidate forum, in answer to a question about the education system and where the parents fit into the scheme of things, I was able to interject something like, "I was talking with Rep. Steve Largent the other night, and he is introducing a Parental Bill of Rights" blah, blah, blah. It is also very informative and absolutely up-to-date.

In fact, I can't say enough about the effort that the NRCC makes to get information to the candidates. Starting at least a year before the election, I received four or five faxes a day on essentially what was going to be in the paper the next day. As the election neared, the stream of data was almost continuous. I could not absorb it all, but it was there if I needed it. I can honestly say that throughout the campaign, I was never caught at a loss for a pertinent answer to a question from an audience or a panelist, and believe me when I say we had some pretty off-the-wall questions.

Of course, there is always one exception. I'm jumping into the campaign when we are talking about pre-campaign activities, but, anecdotally, this story fits here.

Peter Deutsch, my opponent and the incumbent congressman, and I were engaged in one of the few true debates that I was afforded, and it was in the Florida Keys late in the campaign. We were taking turns drawing sealed envelopes containing questions, which the person drawing the question had to answer. The other candidate was then given the opportunity to rebut. Peter drew a question on "wise use". I had never heard the term. I mean, I had devoured everything the NRCC had sent me, I had read columns in the newspaper that I would not normally read, and there was *no issue* that I could not discuss. But I didn't understand this question.

Fortunately, I don't think Peter did either, because he took off on something totally irrelevant, which I did know something about, and I used my rebuttal to attack him on whatever it was he took off on. Someday, I will ask him about that. But, I was glad he drew the question, and not me.

One other thing that I did during this phase of testing the waters was to visit with quite a few of the Freshman Class in order to get their assessments and ideas. To a man, they told me that they needed people with business backgrounds to come to the Congress, and who were willing to serve as "citizen legislators". The consensus was that career politicians had gotten the country into the shape it was in, with a national debt approaching five trillion dollars, and it was going to be up to businesspeople, with a practiced eye toward the "bottom line", to extract the country and put it back on sound financial footing. Not once was I refused a timely meeting, and not once was I discouraged from becoming a candidate. It seems like the Congress, like the U.S. Marine Corps, was *looking for a few good men*

4

TIME TO FISH OR CUT BAIT

Running for national office is not just a personal decision, it is a family decision. In my case, our kids are grown and out of the house. Candy, our oldest, lives in the Washington area and works for Fairfax County. She also has her own business on the side. Paula lives with her husband and young family in New Jersey, and Steve, probably the only nuclear engineering trained mortgage broker in the business, is a very successful mortgage banker in Boynton Beach, Florida. Busily pursuing their own careers, they were not a factor in my decision. My wife, Sandy, was.

We had been separated for eighteen months in a pre-divorce mode while Sandy's attorney undertook the unofficial mandate of re-writing all the divorce Statutes for the State of Florida. We had been back together for only a short while when I decided to run, and I had been in Washington much of that. All of this was very common knowledge, and there was nothing newsworthy in the fact. We were reconciled, but I think we both knew that a political campaign can put a strain on any marriage. There was also the fact that the campaign would be a full-time job, and we would not have much income for six months or so, forcing us to live off of savings.

Although she never said so, I think she would have just as soon I had let it go. But she left the decision up to me and said she would support that decision. She did that.

I also had a 'real-world' problem. During our separation I had bought a condo in the Washington, D.C. area and my intent was to move back there. Even since the reconciliation I was spending almost all my time there on business. I was also trying to sell the condo, and things were not going entirely the way that I had anticipated. The market had cooled considerably and what I had expected to be a "done deal" before Christmas of 1995 had made its way into 1996, forcing me to return to Washington after the holidays. I did not want to be there. I wanted to be in South Florida mounting a campaign. However, my presence there was required, and try as I might, I could not seem to extract myself. I had made the decision that I wanted to run for this seat, but I couldn't do it from Washington. I had to be in Florida.

The filing date for congressional office was in May. As May approached with no solution in sight, I called David Johnson, the Republican Congressional Liaison in Tallahassee, and told him that I had decided to run, that I wanted to run, but that I *couldn't* run. I saw no way that I could be back in Florida in two weeks to meet the filing date, and furthermore, I didn't have the $10,000 required for the filing fee. I had planned to use some of the proceeds from the sale of the condo to get the campaign going, but that just wasn't going to happen.

I also pointed out to David that another Republican candidate had filed, so the seat wouldn't go unopposed. The Republican Party had sworn to cover every single congressional race in the country. He said that the filing date had slipped, due to some mishap in Governor Chiles' office, and that it might be postponed as much as six weeks. He told me to sit tight for a few days, that he had some phone calls to make, and that he would get back to me.

A few nights later Mark Foley, the Republican Congressman from District 16 in Palm Beach and Martin Counties called and said that the party really wanted me to run, and that he wanted me to run. I had met Mark briefly when I called on him while making my rounds talking to Members of the Freshman Class. I also pointed out to him that a candidate from Homestead, Florida had already filed, but Foley said that they didn't know anything about him and that "I was their guy". This made me wonder what they really knew about *me*. My name wasn't exactly a household word. As much as I had traveled out of state and overseas while living in Florida, I probably didn't know over a hundred people there, and most of them had worked for me or with me at some point. Maybe the party had run a background check on me. I'll have to ask David that sometime.

I also told him that I didn't even have the money for the filing fee and he had that covered, as well. He said he had spoken to the NRCC and they were willing to pay it if I would just consent to run. He said he would help me as much as he could, which I knew wouldn't be much insofar as the "non-compete" rule was in effect among the Florida delegation.

Finally, I said that if I could cut a deal on the condo that would free me up, I would do it, but that still looked iffy.

Actually, I had signed a sales contract with a buyer in March and he had put a small down payment on the contract. He had also spent a considerable amount of money making some upgrades on the unit that I had allowed him to make. In the meantime, the buyer had suffered some serious "cash calls" of a personal nature that I knew about and understood, but he had missed some payment milestones. I really liked this man and his wife, and I knew they really wanted the condo, but I was forced to put the property back on the market.

Filing week in Florida had officially been designated as the week of June 21st. Actually, you can file your name anytime, but the five days so designated are the only time you can post the filing fee. If you are going the route of collecting signatures in lieu of paying the fee, all of your signatures must be validated by noon on that fifth day. The amount of signatures required was around 8000 for this particular district. It is a big effort to go this route, but $10,000 is also a hefty fee, one of the most expensive in the country, I am told.

Actually, getting the signatures has its advantages. It gets you out there talking to people and, generally, anyone that signs your filing card will tend to vote for you in the primary and in the general election. This effort is really an extension of your campaign. My plan had originally been to do this, and the thrust of the plan was to recruit fifty or sixty volunteers and station them at various precincts during the Republican Presidential Primary, which occurs in March of the election year. The great thing about this scheme is that you know that everyone coming out of the polling place is: 1) a Republican, 2) a voter, and 3) lives in your district. They are also in a politickin' frame of mind because they have just voted. However, I just didn't have the time to get organized and I really still hadn't made up my mind at that time.

About two weeks before filing week, I called my potential condo buyer and suggested he meet me for a drink. I told him words to the effect that, look, you have defaulted on the sales contract and you have invested a considerable piece of change, which you are going to lose. I'm not interested in making a buck on your misfortune and I want to be out of here and down in Florida getting a campaign going. Go home and come up with a plan that I can live with and you can meet. Get creative, because I can be damned creative if I'm motivated. I was motivated.

He came back with the most convoluted document I had ever seen, and I almost rejected it out-of-hand. However, there were some unique terms and I did some tweaking and faxed it back to him. A couple more similar exchanges and we had an even more convoluted financial document, but it was something I could live with and that he could meet. My son is a mortgage banker and when I showed the agreement to him recently, he just shook his head and said, "Son-of-a-bitch, I've never seen anything like that." But he also couldn't find anything inherently wrong with it. My attorney at the time wouldn't have anything to do with it, but then, lawyers are all deal-killers anyway.

I called both David Johnson and Ann McCord at the NRCC and told them it looked like a "go". Both seemed relieved to hear this and Ann went out of her way to assure me that I was not a "token candidate". She said that my race would probably not be "targeted" (a euphemism for "throwing money at"), but that the NRCC would help all they could.

I've sort of got this thing about the third time someone tells me they are not lying to me I figure they are lying to me. Not that I think Ann would lie, but about the third time that she assured me that I was not a token candidate, I figured I was a token candidate. I knew that the NRCC would go to most any length not to let a race go unchallenged. I accepted that going in, and I knew I was going to be pretty much on my own. I thought I would get a little more help from the party than I did, but I understand why they had to support the ones they did. The election results bear all of this out, and the party obviously made the right decisions, because we still managed to retain control of the Congress, and that is, by far, the most important point.

I also made the decision within myself that I wasn't going to run like a token candidate. I made up my mind to give it my absolute best shot.

I still wasn't out of Washington. My buyer and I had reached an agreement, but nothing had been signed and no money had changed hands. There was a third party involved, whom I had never met, and still haven't. I wasn't leaving town without a "done deal". The deal finally got "done" on June 16th and I was out of there on June 17th to make the filing. I even had to come back at the end of June to actually move out. There were yet to be snags.

The plan was for the NRCC to send the money for the filing fee direct to Tallahassee, where congressional races are filed. On the second of the five filing days, somebody discovered that the rules had changed and the $10,000 had to flow through my campaign account. Fortunately, I had opened a campaign account previously. The NRCC was going to FedEx the check that night and I would deposit it on Wednesday, and FedEx my check to Tallahassee Wednesday night.

Then the NRCC discovered that the most they could give me before the primaries was $5000. Could I come up with the other $5000 and they would reimburse me after the Primary? Unless one is wealthy, it is not wise to put one's own money into a political campaign. It is also a cardinal rule that one doesn't commit retirement funds to a campaign. I am not wealthy, and what funds I have are, in fact, mostly retirement funds, plus we would be living on savings during the campaign. However, I did come up with the $5000. By the time we were able to work through the last minute glitches, it was late Thursday before the elections committee received my filing application and fee. Filing closed at noon on Friday.

It was still very much up in the air whether or not I would have a primary opponent, and I really did not want to go through a primary. The potential candidate from Homestead, Randy Flynn, had still not submitted his signature cards, but he could still come up with the $10,000. The only way I know to approach problems is "straight up". Even though I had never met Randy, I picked up the phone and called him, and said, "Are you running, or not?"

This was Friday morning. He said that he had not been able to get the required number of signatures, and that he was not going to run. There was also an Independent candidate that had filed, but she had not been able to come up with the signatures, either. Actually, I was more worried about her than I was another Republican candidate. The voter registration in this district is 53% Democratic, 35% Republican, and 12% Independent. If I had any chance to win, I was going to need the Independent vote, and I thought I could get it. Ross Perot was out there speaking truth, and I was going to sound a lot like Ross Perot.

That candidate's name is May Choate, and she was more of a "protest candidate" than a serious candidate. Her campaign platform was Term Limits, period, and she said publicly that the only money she intended to spend on the campaign was the money she had spent to have the two tee-shirts made that she and her husband were wearing. She is from Key West. She threw another wrench in the process by filing a suit against the Florida Election Commission for discrimination. The rules require that a candidate either pay the $10,000 filing fee *or* come up with the required number of verifiable signatures. However, for Independent candidates, the requirement is that they do *both*.

I happen to agree with her. This is a double standard. However, the court upheld the criteria and she lost her case. I might add that this ruling did not come down until a week or two before the election. Had she won, it would have been interesting to see how the state could have got all the ballots reprinted, not to mention the absentee ballots that had not only gone out, but many had been received back. The reason for this law is to preclude frivolous candidates from getting on the ballot, I am told. I see nothing frivolous about collecting 8000 signatures *or* coughing up $10,000.

I also want to say a few words about May Choate. She is a delightful lady. I will admit that I didn't particularly want her on the ballot, but after meeting her and her husband, Ray, I decided to keep my mouth shut. I did not do anything to lobby against her being on the ballot. I count her and her husband among the many friends that Sandy and I made during this campaign and I admire her spunk, and I admire her courage for hanging it out there for what she believes. It was a real privilege to have had her as a potential political opponent.

David Johnson called me as soon as their filing period closed and said, "You're it, buddy. You are on the ballot, and You are our candidate in the 20th Congressional District."

5

HEY, Y'ALL WATCH THIS

All kids growing up everywhere do dumb things. This is called just that; "growing up". However, kids growing up in the South *add* a step to this process. They precede the dumb deed by shouting to anyone within earshot, "Hey, y'all watch this"!

The ensuing act is not to be confused with an act of daring. An act of daring involves a definite thought process consisting of the idea, the assessment of the possibility of pulling it off, the value of the reward if it is successfully negotiated, and the consequences if the act fails to culminate in the desired result.

On the other hand a "dumb thing to do" results from having only enough brain cells on-line to trigger the idea. All other brain cells that activate other emotions such as "consequences", "risk factors", "acclaim", and "what-ifs" are out there somewhere harmlessly misfiring. Simply put, in order to yell, "Hey, y'all watch this," your mind has to be a complete blank.

I mention this because, immediately after I hung up the phone with David Johnson, I had this overwhelming urge to shout to everyone present, "Hey, y'all watch this"! Everyone present consisted only of my dog, which was probably just as well.

The next thing that flashed before my eyes was a kaleidoscope of all the dumb things I had ever done. Well, perhaps not *all* the dumb things, because that would not have been a flash, but rather something resembling a slightly abridged version of *War and Remembrance*. But, there were definitely flashbacks and the one I particularly remember took me back to a day when I was perhaps ten or eleven years old.

Cowboys were big in those days, and we played "cowboy" a lot. Bicycles were the primary mode of transportation, whether it was to go to school five miles away or to go next door. We also tried to configure our bicycles to resemble, in both form and function, the horses of our favorite cowboy movie heroes, who we religiously watched every Saturday afternoon at the Rialto Theater. Actually, these configurations were fairly standard, consisting of an Indian blanket, rolled up, tied, and attached behind the seat on the luggage carrier, saddlebags, and a scabbard for a Red Ryder BB gun. This was used to shoot birds off telephone lines, there having been a definite lack of Indians in those days. Furthermore the Animal Rights mavens hadn't worked their way far enough down the food-chain to worry about birds. Of course, there were also streetlights, but taking these out didn't kick in until high school. The BB gun was affixed to the crossbar that delineated a boy's bike from a girl's bike. That's the same bar that tended to make permanent sopranos out of young boys when jumping off the garage onto their bike while emulating their favorite western hero jumping off a saloon roof onto his horse. A lasso, coiled and hung over the handlebars, completed the rigging. It was the latter that figured prominently in this particular flashback.

We had a hill about three miles from where I lived that would rival any hill east of the Rockies. If it had ever snowed in Chattanooga, the airlines would have had to add flights just so skiers could come down that hill. But, it was ours, and we made the trek at least once a week just to go down that hill. It might also be added that to get to the *top* of this hill without going *up* this hill entailed another couple of miles of pedaling by an alternate route. I would guess that something approaching warp speed could be attained going down that hill.

On this particular day, about a third of the way down this hill, I experienced one of the brain farts described above, and decided I would lasso a mailbox near the bottom of the hill. Standing up on the pedals, guiding the bike with one hand, I uncoiled the rope, swung it over my head with a style and flair that Sunset Carson would have died for, and shouted at my cohorts, "Hey, y'all watch this!"

I picked out the mailbox as I was coming out of the hill, threw the loop with a perfect lead, and watched with immense satisfaction as the loop enveloped the mailbox, and took a purchase on the post. It must have been about two microseconds before I became airborne that a couple of those misfiring memory cells timed out and it occurred to me that the end of the lasso was *tied* to my handlebar. I over-flew the second mailbox and hit the third, *with my face*. I still have the scars. They're part of the "rudd".

I have two points: at least back then I was flying straight and level when I hit that mailbox, and henceforth I would be flying upside down much of the time; and I had that same feeling in the pit of my stomach that *always* immediately followed "Hey, y'all watch this"—stark terror.

All of my thinking had been directed at just getting to where I was: on the ballot. It was now that the enormity of the task for which I had just signed up began to dawn on me. Fortunately, after the wild machinations of the past three or four weeks, the period following the filing was almost like a lull. Oh, there were phone calls from various reporters wanting a statement, mainly just wanting to know just who in the hell I was, since no one had ever heard of me. But, at least I had a little time to try and get my act together and to try and put together some form of an organization.

The district itself stretches for two hundred miles from northern Broward County south to the Dade County line. Then it picks up the westernmost portion of Dade County, and I mean westernmost. The part of the Everglades where Valuejet went down is about the geographical center of my Dade district. The district then fishhooks back around and picks up part of East Dade, almost back to Coral Gables. It also includes all of Monroe County, which is basically all of the Florida Keys, all the way to Key West.

There are eight congressional districts in South Florida, most of which having been gerrymandered to some extent. The most convoluted is District 23, Congressman Alcee Hastings' district. This district touches seven counties and is primarily Afro-American. In some places, the district is barely 50 yards wide. My district, which is District 20, was also carefully crafted by Peter Deutsch when he was in the Florida legislature, just before he first ran in the district for his current House seat. It is not drawn by race, but rather by voter registration. The demographics are tough for a Republican candidate, having such a heavy negative partisanship. There are also approximately 400,000 voters in the 20th CD, with 75% of the voters being in Broward County.

All of this began to register with me, now that I was committed. I had a spread-out district, heavy Democratic partisanship, zero name recognition, no political contacts, no organization, no money, and less than four and a half months until the election. I had raised exactly $100, and that had been given to me several months before by a retired FBI agent I had met at one of our hangouts in Crystal City. His name is Bruce Brahe. I hadn't even cashed his check because I had never been quite sure that I was going to run.

I had asked a long time good friend, Ed Clausner, to be my campaign treasurer when I had first opened the campaign account. Ed happened to be on the island of Palau, in the South Pacific, laying underwater cable and would not even be back until late in July. I dare say that no congressional campaign has ever gotten started with less underpinning. If the subject is "starting from scratch", I wrote the book. Come to think of it, I guess this is it.

However, I have always been an optimistic person. Someone once told me that if I fell off a skyscraper, I would probably pass the thirteenth floor thinking, "So far, so good".

In many ways the situation in which I found myself was not a whole lot different than situations in which I had found myself before, especially the two episodes I recounted earlier in this book and that I told you would come to bear. Most salvage jobs are like that. Your first thought is, "How in the hell are we going to walk away from this one?"

I remember the first time that I looked at the scene at that dam on the Arkansas River. My first thought was that there was just no way we were going to be able to save that dam. On the Saudi program, I remember thinking that there was just no way that that program could be turned around. On both occasions, having really no alternative, I just jumped in the middle of it and, with very good people around me, somehow managed to pull it off.

I recall early in the first week Sandy making the remark that we really didn't know anyone who knew the first thing about politics and she was wondering out loud who we were going to get to help us in this campaign. I remember saying to her, "The people that are going to help us the most, we haven't even met yet." This turned out to be prophetic. It was like Ken Follett quoted Ross Perot as saying in the book, "A Flight of Eagles". Key people, or "eagles", as Perot calls them, don't congregate; you have to find them one at a time. When you find one, you latch onto him.

Actually, I had already found my first "eagle"; I just didn't know it, and she was right under my nose. Sandy has never been particularly political, but she has not been an uninformed voter, either. She tends to vote for the "person", and we have canceled a few of each other's votes over the years. I never dreamed how involved she would become in this campaign, doggedly attending candidate forums, trips to the Keys, whatever it took. I even had to wrestle her for the political section of the paper every morning, as she became very knowledgeable about the issues.

She also played very well in the Keys, and probably could have gotten more votes there than I did. She became my harshest critic, and very quickly developed excellent political instincts. However, the first thing we had to do was to change her political affiliation. She was a Democrat, for Christ's sake. In fact, she was probably the only Democrat at Presidency III. Well, at least she wasn't a delegate. Come to think of it, she was probably the only registered Democrat at the Republican candidate school. Furthermore, the day we had our picture taken with Gingrich, he commented to her how much he liked her dress. If *that* hadn't sent her running down to the Supervisor of Elections for a Transfer of Party Affiliation Card, I figured nothing ever would.

Our first official function was the Greater Plantation 4th of July Parade. Actually a parade is no big deal, but when you get a call asking you to be in it on July 3rd, it *becomes* a big deal. I had to get magnetic signs made for the convertible so everyone along the parade route would know what the hell I was doing *in* the parade. I also had to find a convertible. South Florida has a lot of rental cars, but try to find a convertible on July 3rd. My fingers wore out the Yellow Pages before I finally found a drug-money laundering outfit fronting as a rental car company that had just one left. Almost as an afterthought, it occurred to us that we needed a driver. A *Candidate* can't just drive himself. Fortunately, we had some friends, Pixie Wright and Bob Brindley, who have a somewhat warped sense of humor, and who not only agreed to drive us, but also agreed to get up at 5 AM in order to do so. This allowed Sandy and me to sit on the back of the rear seat and do the old grin-and-wave trick while throwing candy at the kids along the parade route. Kissing babies will now get you five to ten, but it's still OK to chuck candy at them.

We even had our dog with us. When your kids have come to the conclusion that you are entering the early stages of senility and refuse to participate in the furtherance thereof, you work with what you've got. Of course, the dog fell out of the convertible about half way through the parade and everything behind us ground to a screeching halt while I retrieved her. How's this guy going to help lead the nation when he does a dog-drop in front of a thousand flag-waving voters?

The first thing that happened in this early part of the campaign was that everyone with something to sell came beating on my door, and everyone who had an agenda congregated around. One fellow, who will remain anonymous, had grandiose ideas, endless enthusiasm, boundless energy, and of course an agenda. He showed up at our house with a brand new 37 foot mobile home with a driver for touring the district, laid out a publicity campaign that included everything from sky-writing to getting the recently defeated Israeli Prime Minister Peres over here to help us with the Jewish vote. He found me a "free" campaign office, and even painted it himself before I had even seen a lease, which turned out to be available for $600 a month. He arranged for phone banks, computers and copiers, and was running around to all the political caucuses dropping my name and spouting my positions on everything from gays in the military to Whitewater, neither one of which I intended to touch. He also wanted to be a paid staffer, so he could put his business on hold and work for me full time. I told him that sure, we can do all of that; just go out and raise me $20,000 and be back here in two weeks and we'll put all of this in motion. I never heard from him again.

A local PR firm laid out a plan which would have cost about $50,000 over a four month period, but, unlike the example above, these guys were legitimate and I undoubtedly needed what they were selling. I just couldn't afford it, and I was not going to get into obligations which I had no idea whether or not I could meet. We remained friends, and they did give me some free advice from time to time, and I'm sure they could have helped me immensely. I simply didn't have the luxury.

In the meantime, I needed to raise money. I had had the foresight to at least have some campaign stationary printed while I was "testing the waters" and I sat down and made a list of everyone I had ever known in my entire life. I invested $40 on a CD-ROM residential telephone directory for the entire United States and got real chummy with the mail-merge feature on my computer. Most campaigns had volunteer staffs to do this stuff. In this campaign, I did it.

Remember my high school fraternity, the Commodores? I had been back to Montgomery, Alabama a year or so earlier for the first ever fraternity reunion. This was the first time I had seen any of these guys in over forty years. They all got a letter. One of the more meaningful things that happened in this campaign was that most of them responded with a contribution. A hundred dollars here, a hundred dollars there, it wasn't much, but at least we were off the ground, and I will never forget them for this.

I also wrote to heavy Republican political contributors in Broward. Nothing. Zip! With very few exceptions, what money I raised was raised in $50 and $100 increments. I had a few $500 contributions and even a very few for $1000, but, by and large, it was grassroots all the way. My first "official" contribution in response to my initial letter was from Al DeAngelus, a former Assistant Commissioner for Enforcement Support at the U.S. Customs Service, whom I had met through a mutual friend. He consented to serve on my campaign executive committee as my advisor on law enforcement. Al also made a follow-up contribution in the closing days of the campaign when I was scurrying around trying to raise money for TV time. If I run again, he will certainly be a player. A former business mentor and friend, Gil Maton, sent me $500, as did my son, Steve.

Probably the most meaningful contribution that I received came from my sister, Gail, late in the campaign. It was for a thousand dollars; money I know she and her husband, Ron, don't have to throw around. When I called her, she said that the money had come from an insurance policy that my dad had paid up for her many years ago. He has been dead for over twenty years. It was as if he was supporting me from on high somewhere. It really touched me. I think both of my parents would have been proud of what the prodigal son that had caused them so much grief as a teenager was trying to do. Actually, I think my parents taught me a good sense of values, but very little else. My Dad wasn't athletic and he was not very handy around the house, but he did teach me the work ethic. About the only thing else he taught me was to never play poker with anyone named "Doc", never gamble at golf with a guy with a good tan and a one-iron in his bag, and when looking for a place to eat in a strange town, never eat at a place called "Moms" unless the only other place to eat has a sign out front that says "Eats".

Then eat at "Moms". But, what the hell, that will at least keep you alive, healthy, and reasonably solvent. Of one thing I am absolutely sure; never in his wildest dreams would my Dad ever have thought that the money from that policy would be used to buy TV air time for a congressional campaign. Thank you, Gail and Ron; and thank you, Dad.

I found my second "eagle" and it *was also* someone we already knew. Marcia Noble is a very good friend of my wife, and a Canadian citizen. Not even able to vote, Marcia became one of my biggest supporters and a tireless worker. Hardly a day went by that she didn't call and say, "I got three more votes today", or two, or four. She wore my T-shirts, carried my campaign literature everywhere she went, wore my campaign button, used my campaign sign as a "sun shield" every time she parked her car, and kept our dog when we had to run down to the Keys. I think every vote she got was a Democrat vote, those being the best kind. Furthermore, she was so absolutely sure that I was going to pull this thing off that her attitude became infectious. We had our good days and our bad days. There were no bad days when Marcia was around.

Once the initial burst of contribution letters were in the mail, there was the formality of making an official announcement of the campaign. I don't know where this inane ceremonial rite sprang roots but I was heavily pressured by some members of the Republican Executive Committee to rent a hotel ballroom, hire caterers, invite the press and TV, and make a big splash. I regarded it merely as something to get past. I made some mistakes in this campaign, but low-keying this passage wasn't one of them.

After much soul searching, I decided to hold the official announcement at the City of Plantation Historical Society's Museum. There were two reasons for this selection. First, Marcia was the President of the Museum, and she offered it free, but the compelling reason was the significance of the site. The museum links Plantation to the past and I wanted to stress the changes that had taken place in Broward County in the twenty years I had lived there, emphasizing the political changes that were about to take place, because my intent was *to win this election*, something no other Republican had ever been able to do in West Broward. It was a fitting ceremony attended by a few close friends and the appropriate local Republican leadership. I think we got through the whole thing for under $50 and the press didn't show up anyway. It was one of my better calls.

My first campaign crisis, of which there would be several, reared its head about this time. My Treasurer was in the South Pacific, as I mentioned earlier, but he had dropped off the checkbook, statements, and the FEC manuals before he left the country. I knew there were stringent reporting requirements required by the FEC, and on Friday the 12th of July, I decided I had better take a look at the requirements. To my absolute horror, it seemed the report was due in Washington on Monday, the 15th, which meant that I had to have it in FedEx hands that day. The FEC is very unforgiving on late filings.

If one can imagine a hypothetical situation of never, ever having filed an income tax return and having to sit down and file one from scratch in a little over six hours, my immediate problem might be understood. Furthermore, I had no forms, and I didn't even know what forms I needed. Since this was the first time that filing was required, there were no previous forms to go by. I made a rather frantic call to the FEC in Washington and stated my problem.

Fortunately, the FEC has its act together. They not only faxed me the forms, but they gave me a phone number whereby one can order forms by computer, in case I managed to screw those up. I managed to screw those up.

I got all this done, but in the course of so doing, I managed to get one number in the wrong box. This error did not affect the bottom line whatsoever. In fact, when the error was caught, my treasurer was back on the job and was not even required to file an amended report. All we had to do was write a two sentence letter explaining what happened. I only mention this here, but it will take on significance later.

One of the first reporters that I talked to during filing week was Rick Van Grouw, of the Key West Citizen, the daily newspaper of the Keys. He asked me all the usual questions on why I was running and what were the major issues that I planned to stress. He also brought up local issues that were on the minds of voters in the Keys. Of course, I was up on the national issues, but I had spent very little time in South Florida during the past eighteen months, and I was not up on the Florida Keys issues. I told him this. He mentioned the Florida Keys National Marine Sanctuary and an issue about the Federal Emergency Management Agency (FEMA) threatening to withhold flood insurance coverage in the Keys to homeowners with non-conforming lower level enclosures on their houses. I asked him to brief me on both issues and he did. I also told him that I would study the issues and get back to him.

One of the many things they taught us in Candidate's School was never to try and bullshit the press. Say you don't know, but that you will find out and get back to them, and then *do it*! I did this and Rick wrote a nice piece on me, but the Sanctuary issue loomed as the major issue in the campaign in Monroe County, one on which I desperately needed to get a handle.

My wayward treasurer was still in the South Pacific and he and his wife own a time-share condominium in Key West for the week of July 13. They offered it to us. Sandy and I saw this as a great opportunity to not only kick off our campaign in the Keys, but to get up to speed on the FEMA and Sanctuary issues.

Just before we went down to the Keys, I received several phone calls. One was from Bettye Chaplin, a Realtor in Marathon, in the Central Keys, who said she would like to meet me and possibly work on my campaign. She added that she was a Democrat.

Another was from Joe Bell, the publisher of a Keys newsletter, the Oracle. Joe and I talked for about a half hour. In fact, it is hard to talk with Joe Bell for anything less than a half hour. He is a retired U.S. Army helicopter pilot, who served in Vietnam. Joe obviously didn't like Peter Deutsch. In fact, not liking Deutsch in the Keys is a popular sport. I told him I was coming down and would like to meet him. Joe told me, "Jim, I'm pretty controversial. You don't want to get too close to me". He did agree to fax me a copy of his newsletter.

Well, I've been known to be controversial myself, "mercurial" being a term applied more than once. I liked what he had to say in his news-letter, and I liked the way he said it. There is no mistaking where Joe Bell is coming from. I wrote Joe a follow-up letter to the phone call and told him that unless he just refused to meet with me, I still wanted to meet him.

The third call I got was from a Vietnam Purple Heart recipient, John Donnelly. John is a Monroe County teacher, an NRA member, and a Republican activist. John also wanted to support me and we agreed to meet.

The Monroe County Republican Executive Committee was having their monthly meeting in Marathon the day we planned to go to Key West, and I agreed to speak at that meeting on the way down. I also set up a meeting with Bettye Chaplin while in Marathon, on the way to Key West. Another call I made was to Dan Probert in Key West. Dan is a recently retired Navy civil servant, who has been a customer of mine for over twenty years, and knows almost everyone in the Lower Keys. I told him that Sandy and I were going to be in town for a week and would like to meet with as many potential supporters as we could. He agreed to meet with us and to help us.

The week we spent early in the campaign in Key West was probably the single, most productive week we spent in the entire campaign. There are a lot of "eagles" in the Keys.

We made the meeting with the Monroe County Executive Com-mittee and found them to be a very cohesive group. We also had the chance to meet many of the Republican candidates for various offices in Monroe County, who were at the meeting. We would be seeing a lot of all of them in the coming months.

I picked up my third "eagle" with Bettye Chaplin. Bettye is a registered Democrat and a prolific political activist. She also is no fan of Peter Deutsch. Sandy and I hit it off with her immediately. She liked what I had to say and I liked what she had to say. She is also very active in the Conch Coalition, the group most opposed to the Marine Sanctuary, and she provided a complete briefing on the Sanctuary. She also invited us back up to Marathon later in the week to attend a meeting of the Conch Coalition, which we did attend.

Dan Probert, true to his word, invited us to a Navy League luncheon in Key West and to a meeting of the Civilian Advisory Committee breakfast with the Key West Navy Detachment there. Debbie Horan, the Democratic State Senator, was the guest speaker, but even more important, her brother-in-law, Attorney David Horan, another Sanctuary foe, became my fourth "eagle". Dave is probably the most articulate and well-versed opponent of the Sanctuary in the Florida Keys. He is also the past President of the Key West Chamber of Commerce. He gave me by far the best briefing on the Florida Keys National Marine Sanctuary that I had received to date. The issue was highly charged with emotion on both sides. Pushing for the Sanctuary was the government, led by Deutsch and the environmentalists. Lining up against the Sanctuary was the Conch Coalition and many of the business leaders and property owners. The hard-core environmentalists are basically knee-jerkers, and the Conch Coalition had a fair dose of emotionalism, as well. The cool head, as far as I could identify it, was Horan. There were other prominent citizens, equally well versed on the local issues, working both sides, but I just did not have the time to get to meet them all. Even though Dave and I didn't totally agree on all aspects of the question, we certainly agreed in principle, and we became, and remain allies on the issue.

We need to talk about this issue, because I think it has national ramifications. It certainly has ramifications for the future of the Florida Keys. In 1990, the U.S. Congress passed the Florida Keys National Marine Sanctuary (FKNMS) Act designating the Florida Keys Barrier

Reef to be a national treasure and in need of protection. So far; so good. Hardly anyone could argue with that.

Congress designated the Commerce Department as the Administrative Agency to put the Act into effect. Commerce, in turn, designated the National Oceanographic and Atmospheric Agency (NOAA) as the Sanctuary administrative arm. NOAA was given two years to come up with a management plan that Congress and the State of Florida would ratify. NOAA enlisted The Nature Conservancy (TNC) to help in formulating the management plan and to "educate" the citizens of Monroe County relative to all the wonderful things that having the Sanctuary would mean for the Florida Keys.

As is usually the case when the government gets involved in any program, the program tends to grow exponentially and the government tends to run amok, especially where there is a tendency for the program to infringe upon individual property rights. A mitigating factor was also involved in this particular issue, I believe, and that is the fact that the Department of Commerce had become a candidate for elimination under the new Republican Congress. This theory is entirely my own, but I think this factor caused NOAA to become even more motivated to build an empire in the Florida Keys using the Sanctuary Act as a cornerstone. Actually, this is not a bad plan for a bureaucrat. If your job is going to be trashed in Washington, the Keys is not a bad place to feather your new nest.

As is also the case when the government is charged with producing a comprehensive plan to do most anything, deadlines are ignored and milestones are missed. It took over four years to get a draft plan on the street and by then the FKNMS had expanded geographically from the original reef tract to a 2800 square mile area reaching from mean high tide on the shoreline, or individual seawalls, out to a water depth of 300 feet. It also extended all the way to the Dry Tortugas, most of the area lying within international waters. Correspondingly, the management plan had grown to a three volume, 800 page diatribe of open-ended powers and regulations, undefined and unstated user fee schedules, a disturbing propensity for levying fines on unwary, or unlucky, violators, and an absolutely frightening power to regulate and restrict runoff from adjacent property into the Sanctuary, over which an individual property owner might have little or no control and which might well have an adverse effect on property values in the Keys.

Aside from the insidious threat to the rights of property owners in the Florida Keys, the biggest problem I had with the Sanctuary was the fact that the original intent, as proposed in 1990, was to protect the barrier reef, the only living coral reef in the contingent United States, from ship groundings and from the effects from offshore oil exploration and drilling. Nowhere in the government produced management plan was there any provision for either of these issues. In fact, under NOAA guidance, or at least on their watch, the Coast Guard had removed vital navigational aids from the area, which would tend to make it more likely that ships plying the waters off the Florida Keys could conceivably tend to run aground on the reef, and in so doing, spill oil.

This encroachment finally began to dawn on the residents of Monroe County and they managed to get a non-binding referendum on the General Election ballot. Even this took a lot of doing and a lot of hard work by the Conch Coalition and some county officials. At this point, I think many of the residents of the Keys still favored a Sanctuary for the reef tract, but the framers of the referendum, at the insistence of the government, for whatever reason, insisted on playing hardball. The only two choices that would appear on the ballot were; YES: I want the Sanctuary, and NO: I don't want the Sanctuary.

My immediate tendency was to back the Conch Coalition, mainly because I had been down similar roads with the federal government over the years, and I could see a huge bureaucracy being forced down the throats of the residents. There were just too many unanswered questions. Once in-place, there would be no recourse, and I inherently do not like situations where there is no "Plan B". Furthermore, the cornerstone of my campaign was for a lot less government, and this was anything but. However, in July as I was coming up to speed on these issues, the polls were showing that the Sanctuary issue would pass by a 60% to 40% margin. I still wanted to jump into the fray.

At the insistence of Bettye Chaplin, Dave Horan, and others whose political instincts I tended to trust, I remained uncommitted. The only way I was going to win this election would be to take 75% of the vote in the Keys. I was also advised by the Republican leadership in the Keys not to let myself become too involved in this particular issue. Reluctantly, I agreed to hold off for a while.

Another "eagle" who surfaced about this time was Carl Haggenkotter. Carl heads up the "Victims of NOAA" and he is also a columnist for the Chronicle, a small Florida Keys newspaper. Carl can best be described as a "coconut chucker", and I certainly mean no disrespect by this. He is probably the fiercest opponent to the Sanctuary in the Keys, and was the most constant thorn in the side of the Sanctuary supporters as there was there. He also busted his butt for me down there putting up signs, arranging a rally, and raising money. If I had to name the one person who worked the hardest for me in this campaign, it would be Carl.

Other supporters that we met during this week in the Keys were Harry Sawyer, the Monroe County Supervisor of Elections, and his wife, Mary, who was the Monroe County Republican Executive Committeewoman. Mary later became my campaign manager in the Keys. Harry probably runs one of the best election operations in the country. He walked me through it while we were there. It is totally electronic, and virtually tamper-proof. Reporting is done by modem, and he said he would have the complete results on election night one hour after the polls closed, and he did.

Another couple that we met and liked was Larry Blocher and his wife, Toni. Larry is retired Army and he and Toni publish a military newsletter, the Southernmost Military Times. Larry served on my campaign Executive Committee as Advisor on Military Affairs.

During this week in Key West, I had to drive all the way back up to Ft. Lauderdale to attend a Broward Executive Committee meeting. I was pretty much "directed" to be there because I was a candidate and very few of the membership had even met me.

Furthermore, Jeb Bush was going to be the speaker, and I wanted to meet him. On the way back I stopped in Key Largo and met with John Donnelly, picking up another "eagle". John is an NRA activist, and he campaigned diligently in my behalf throughout the campaign. He also built and installed my campaign signs between the Upper Keys and Marathon, and he tirelessly made a half dozen trips to South Miami for our Wednesday night strategy meetings.

On the way back down the following day, I stopped again in Key Largo and met Joe Bell, the crusty publisher of the Oracle. Joe has a refreshing policy with his newsletter. He will not accept contributions from candidates and he will not place anyone on his mailing list unless they call him and personally request that he do so. I would surmise that everyone who receives the newsletter, reads it. We swapped war stories, found that our backgrounds were similar in many ways, and became friends. Joe supported me unfailingly in his publication, and became my "ears" in the Upper Keys, looking out for my interests on several occasions. We still talk about playing some golf together, and now that the election is over, maybe we will get the chance. We both purport to carry a thirteen handicap, but Joe is such a sandbagger I would probably have to uncork a 74 or 75 to beat him.

While I was back in Ft. Lauderdale, Sandy and some friends of ours, Dave and Renie Bayer covered for me at another Republican meeting in the Keys that I was unable to attend. Dave got up and went over my platform, having memorized it from the campaign issue cards that I had been handing out. I think Dave is a Democrat so this must have been painful, but he did it anyway. He also introduced Sandy to the group. Of course, those present thought it appropriate that they hear a few words from the candidate's wife. Sandy wasn't quite ready for "Prime Time Live", but she handled it pretty well. She stood up and said, "Jim and I have an agreement. Whoever's picture is on this card does all the talking." And as she held up the "issue card" with only my picture on it, she added, "You don't see my picture on this card." Later, I added her picture on these cards.

The week ended with a large reception of all the Monroe County candidates, this being the last day to file for county races. Sandy's effectiveness became apparent to me because she knew a lot of people there that I didn't know and that she had met during my short absence. She was a very big hit in the Keys, and even more important, she was starting to "get into it". We also picked up another "eagle".

Mel Fisher, the renowned treasure hunter, was at this reception. Mel is one of the most popular men in the Keys and is known as the "King Conch". He has been jerked around unmercifully by our government relative to the disposition of various treasures he has found. Found at great personal sacrifices, I might add. Since I had also been in the salvage business, although not for treasure, we found that we had a lot in common. The Sanctuary did not promise to do much for him, nor for anyone making their living on the water, and he was active in the opposition to the issue. He would prove to be a major supporter, both financially and otherwise, in the days ahead. We came out of the Keys the following day with a lot of new friends, a semblance of an organization there, and a good handle on the local issues, especially on the Florida Keys National Marine Sanctuary. I sensed we could win big in the Keys.

Meanwhile, back to reality. Of course, the mailbox was full, and what it was full of would become a time-consuming campaign chore to be dealt with. Questionnaires. Every Special Interest Group and organization known to man must send out questionnaires to congressional candidates. Some organizations, such as the Eagle Forum and the Christian Coalition, have as many as fifty questions. Others have as few as five questions. Some of the organizations I had never heard of, and others embraced issues with which I was totally unfamiliar.

Here's one from the National Committee of Armenia:

Do you support the Freedom Support Act restriction on U.S. aid to Azerbaijan and will you oppose any efforts to weaken or eliminate this ban until Azerbaijan has lifted its blockade and ended its aggression against Nagorno Karabagh and Armenia?

Well, that one sure as hell wasn't on the list of "Fifty Questions I Had Better Be Able to Answer" that the NRCC had sent me before I got into this thing. While some of these organizations will send you money if they like your answer, they all send out voter's guides to their membership, and the number of voters that vote from such guides is incredible. This particular question, and others from the same group, sent me to the library. I am naturally curious and always anxious to learn something new, but in the heat of a campaign when *time* is not your friend, many of these questionnaires can be extremely time consuming. I don't think I ducked a one, and I'm sure I answered well over a hundred, even those that I knew I must answer truthfully with a "wrong" answer.

News organizations, national magazines, political publications, such as the Congressional Quarterly, and other print media also make strong demands on your time for background information and issue statements. Many of these will see print only if you are successful in winning your election. Others, such as Time magazine, print a voter's guide that appears just before the election. Of course, all of these requests also want you to include a picture.

One of the smartest things I did was to put a Web Site on the Internet. If you think about it, not many individuals had their own personal web sites in 1966. Like everything else, the costs of doing this varied widely. I had estimates as high as $2000. I settled on a little two-man company called Digital Document Corporation, run by two ex-schoolmates of my son and both of whom I had known for years. I also had them do some printing for me, but they charged me less than $200 for a professionally done Web Site. Of course, I provided all the copy on disc, but the site consisted of color photographs, a color photo "Album" that I could add to or subtract from, a "Hot Topic" section that I could access from my own computer to change copy, and over eighteen pages of single spaced typewritten copy, which tells more about me, my family, my business background, and my military service than anyone would ever want to know. It also covered major issues with two-liners expandable to multi-paragraph with a click of the mouse.

This was extremely handy when these news organizations requested background data. I would merely point them to the Web Site and tell them to call me back if they still needed anything. No one ever called back except to tell me what a great Web Site I had. We finally put a counter on the site, but this wasn't done until right before the election. I have no idea how many hits I had, but I had quite a few in the closing days.

Probably the toughest questionnaires to complete were from the Ft. Lauderdale Sun-Sentinel and the Miami Herald. Both were requested prior to the respective candidate interview, and each took well over eight hours for me to complete.

When a candidate starts from scratch, as I did, with no political experience whatsoever, and with no campaign manager or other credible advisor, everything carries a learning curve. Even simple things like campaign literature (handouts) and bumper stickers become a challenge. Just before we went to the Keys for the week, I thought that it would be a great idea to take bumper stickers down with me and pass them out. What a great place for bumper stickers. In the Keys, everyone runs up and down U.S. 1 everyday and you are always behind somebody. How many to buy would be a recurring problem with everything I bought, but this time that wasn't the problem because I only had money for 1000. Apparently, that was enough because I'm still trying to get rid of the damn things. It seems people don't like to put the stickers on the plastic bumpers of the new cars because they tend to peel off the paint. People will take them, but they won't put them on their cars. I went through at least 800 bumper stickers in the

Keys, and I don't think I ever saw one of my stickers on a car down there.

Campaign literature, handouts, issue cards, whatever one wants to call them, were another learning curve. I designed my cards, and I had a lot of complements on them. Consequently, I made very few changes, but I had no idea how many I would need. My first buy was for a thousand. I had no idea how many that really was, and when I got them I didn't see how I would ever use them all. Then I bought another thousand, and then two thousand, and then three thousand. Finally I bought 10,000, and with less that a month to go before the election, I bought 20,000. I could have made a substantial savings if I had just bought 40,000 on my first buy. When one thinks about it, that is really not many cards; only one for every ten voters in the district.

When I first realized that I was the Republican nominee, and on the ballot for the general election, I was elated that I didn't have to go through a primary election. I also came to learn that primaries are incongruous, and I will try to explain that observation.

For a Republican to face a primary in a district such as this, it would be necessary to spend much of your time and money just to win the primary. Having done that, you would only have a month to campaign against the Democratic opponent, with that opponent having a big edge in voter registration. I felt that my chances were much better without a primary in that I could start from Day One running against Deutsch. That was fallacy number 1. In the District 19 race, immediately to the north of this district, it was an open seat race and both parties had a primary.

The three Democratic candidates in that heavily Democratic district were all highly qualified, experienced politicians. All three had resigned State seats, two from the State Senate and one from the State House in order to seek this open seat. The winner of the primary would probably coast into office by virtue of the voter registration demographics. Of the two Republican candidates, Beverly Kennedy easily won her primary, mainly because her opponent was unqualified. But she was beaten badly in the general election.

In retrospect, I would probably have been better off if I had had a primary. What I needed more than anything was name recognition, and to get that with my very meager resources, I needed "earned media", which is another one of those euphemisms meaning press coverage. However, all the action was in the Democratic primary in District 19 where the three Democrats were beating each other's brains out. You name it, they had it all; personal attacks, negative mail-outs, lawsuits, the whole spectrum. Naturally, they received all the media coverage. Beverly Kennedy, the Republican candidate in that race, got some coverage fallout from all this, but not much. That was really the "only game in town" until after the primaries, when attention turned to the other races. But from late June until early September, I don't think I could have gotten a column inch if I had been slapped with a DUI.

In this particular race it probably didn't matter very much because I was having a much harder time raising money than I had anticipated. With nothing much happening, I was able to concentrate on raising money, and I wasn't spending any. However, if I should ever decide to do this again, it will be with a lot more money, and in that case, I'm not sure I would mind having a primary.

The other thing I was able to do was to sharpen my public speaking skills by attending as many Candidate Forums as possible. I have always been an adequate speaker, but I have never been a good public speaker. Furthermore, I have never had much of an occasion to hone these skills. Of course, I had given a few technical papers, and I had presided at business meetings, briefed our Board of Directors, and given technical and marketing pitches to customers and potential customers. But I had never been in any kind of adversarial scenario, which, of course, is exactly what a political campaign is. I call this view-with-alarm-point-with-pride-and-poison-the-well speaking opportunities.

Candidate Forums were beginning to be scheduled by civic clubs, homeowner's associations, political clubs, business clubs, and you name it. Candidate Forums are also a dichotomy. On one hand they are a pain in the ass, but on the other hand, these forums give one the opportunity to try out some lines, fine-tune your issues, and develop your style for the TV debates which will come after the primaries, and which *are* important. It was preparing for some of these that I found another "eagle".

My dentist, Dr. Richard Keller, had called me soon after I announced my candidacy and told me that his seventeen year-old son was heavily into politics and would like to work on my campaign. He suggested I give him a call if I had anything for him to do. Frankly, I had no idea what I could do with a seventeen year-old high school student, but I liked Richard and I gave the kid a call and asked him to drop over. His name is Ashley, and he came by and we chatted. I asked him what he would like to do, and he said he would do anything just to work on a congressional campaign. He said he would drive or even stuff envelopes, although he didn't seem too overly excited about the latter. He did mention in passing that he was the current national high school political debating champion. Aha! I was scheduled to speak at a meeting of the Southwest Broward Republican Club the following evening and I asked him to be there and to critique my speech.

I write my own speeches. I have tried to give somebody else's speech and I just can't do it unless I read it, and *I will not read a speech.* I find that if I write it, I write it in my style of speaking, and then I can deliver it the way I wrote it. I had written a fifteen-minute speech for this group and I was comfortable with it, and I thought I did a pretty fair job delivering it, especially when I didn't notice Ashley taking any notes, right? Wrong!

He came by the next day, and as deferential as a seventeen year old kid critiquing a congressional candidate can possibly be, he proceeded to very politely tear me apart. I will spare the reader all the gory details, but under Ashley's guidance I very quickly became a much better speaker. Without asking him, I made him a member of my Campaign Executive Committee, had his name added to my campaign stationary as "Communications Advisor", and sent him a note on the new stationary that said, "This will look good on your resume." He was elated.

I used Ashley as a stand-in for several candidate forums when there was a scheduling conflict. The feedback always came back with words to the effect, "Where did you find that guy?" I will get back to this "eagle" later, because I have more to say about this young man.

Another decision I made during this period of waiting for the primaries to be decided was to just try and be myself. It is very easy to get swept up in the fact that you are running for the U.S. Congress, and I decided that if I wasn't careful, I was going to start to take myself seriously. This is not to say that I wasn't going to take the campaign seriously, but politicians tend to sound stiff and pontifical. That is not my style. I have always prided myself on having a good sense of humor and I think a little humor has a place anywhere, including a political campaign. *Especially including a political campaign.* Wherever I could, I tried to work a little humor into my speeches, especially when taking questions from the floor. Anytime that I could I tried to get out from behind the podium and hold the mike in my hard. This was not always convenient, but it made me more comfortable and it made it easier to talk *"with"* the audience. I also promised Betty Clausner, the wife of my campaign treasurer, that I would not publicly use the 'f' word under any circumstances for the duration of the campaign. In the same vein, I promised Sandy that I would try not to call anyone an asshole. I fell a little short on the latter. This was tough because it is one of my favorite descriptive phrases. I remember the Seventies when there was a constant rash of aircraft hi-jackings to Cuba. It was during this time that I was frequently flying up and down the East Coast, always with an attache case full of Secret documents related to my work. Sandy constantly reminded me, "Now, if you get hi-jacked to Cuba, don't call anyone an asshole. Oh, and here's a list of things I want you to get me while you're on the ground there."

I also found that talk radio was a good medium for me. The first show that I was on was with Nat Treger. Nat is a Republican, and when we first talked on the phone he assured me that he would be a "friendly" interviewer, and he was. But it really wasn't necessary. I was well up on all the issues and I liked answering questions. When you give a speech to an audience in a political forum, you hope that you are addressing the concerns of the audience. When you are taking questions, you know that you are addressing their concerns because they asked the questions.

I also had the opportunity to be on "Adam's World", with Adam Clatsoff, on a couple of occasions. "Captain Truth", as he calls himself, is a poor man's Rush Limbaugh, although he is a registered Democrat. I really enjoyed these shows because Adam *does* speak the truth. He is also a close personal friend of Peter Deutsch, and he told me that up-front, but I never felt intimidated by it. I think the thing I enjoyed most with Adam is that he is a free thinker. He has a tendency to lead you way out on a limb with a series of profound, obscure ideas that you had probably never even thought about but with which you didn't totally disagree. Then he would say, "What do you think about that"? It was then up to me to get back on firm ground before the limb broke from my own weight. He did this to me on more than one occasion and far from being offended, I found it mentally stimulating. You don't go on Adam's show with a canned set of points you want to tick off. You have to make your points within the framework that he gives you to work with. However, having made your point in this manner, it is much more effective.

Basically, it is against FEC rules to "campaign" on talk radio or TV unless your opponent appears with you. This is viewed as free airtime and if it is made available to you, it must also be made available to the other candidates in your race. This is a very thin line and it is probably skirted more than any other election rule. Many talk show hosts get around it by agreeing to invite any candidate who calls and requests to be on the show, thus making the airtime available. There is also the question of where does the discussion of one's position on certain issues end and "campaigning" begin. This is why I like Adam's format and his manner in dealing with his guests. He seems to raise political issues more to a level of intellectual discussion rather than the appearance of pure campaigning.

The fact that his program is in the morning, and I am not necessarily a morning person, made it even more of a challenge, but it sure got my day going.

Adam has told me twice that whenever he goes out of town, I can do his show as a guest host. One of these days I think I will take him up on it.

There are a number of problems with candidate forums. On the upside, I think that any group that has enough interest in getting their membership educated on the issues deserves the courtesy of the candidate's attendance. Likewise, I feel that any member of that group that shows up in an effort to become familiar with the issues and the individual candidate's position on these issues deserves to hear that candidate, or at least hear the candidate's surrogate.

On the downside, there are many candidates on the ballot and time must be strictly controlled or the forum could run all night. Sandy and I have left a forum at 1:30 in the morning and still faced fifty miles to drive home. Most forums allow each candidate a maximum of three minutes to introduce themselves and to state their platform, or priorities. They may or may not allow questions from a panel or from the floor. Three minutes may be ample for the Mosquito Control Board, but it is woefully inadequate to discuss national issues, especially when that is the only shot you get at that particular audience. There are also those forum sponsors that may boast a 600-person membership, but only twenty -five members show up. I probably participated in thirty candidate forums, and in a few of them, the candidates outnumbered the audience. In fact, there is not a candidate that ran in either Broward or Monroe Counties for whom I could not attend in their stead as a surrogate and give their speech, so many times have I heard them.

Furthermore, in these thirty or so forums, I probably reached less than 700 voters, less than 2/10th of one percent of the voters in my district.

That my performance improved on the public speaking circuit by a couple orders of magnitude was partly due to Ashley, partly due to me, but was also partly due to chemicals. No, this is not going to be a bombshell. Early in the campaign, I took my annual physical exam and I mentioned to our family doctor of over twenty years that, with as much public exposure as I had had, and as comfortable as I was with the subject matter that I was discussing, I still had a "tightness" when I got up before a group. As much as I enjoy being "on", and as confident as I was in what I had to say, I still seemed to get this adrenaline rush that seemed to affect my breathing. He informed me that this was known as "stage fright", and he told me that many veteran actors and actresses experienced this after years on the stage or in front of a camera. He also said there was an effective "cure" for this condition, and he prescribed Inderal. The way he described the effect of the drug was to imagine almost having a head-on collision in a car, barely missing the other car, and expecting the tremendous adrenaline rush that would immediately follow. On Inderal that rush would not occur. It is a beta-blocker and it is prescribed for people with very high blood pressure or a heart condition that doesn't need such stress as caused by a sudden release of adrenaline.

He went on to say that taking one pill an hour before a "performance" would eliminate the problem. He also said that the medication does not precipitate a drugged effect and, if anything, tends to make one become a bit sharper.

I tried it and it works like a charm. Deutsch and I got into some fairly intense debates in the final stages of the campaign, and I stayed totally loose and composed. About half way through the campaign, I intentionally neglected to take the pill, and my performance suffered. I don't leave home without it on the campaign trail. If Peter reads this and I face him again, he will probably claim that I am on drugs.

Another thing that I did before the primaries was to develop a "capture plan". Usually this should be done as part of the "testing the waters" phase of a campaign, but, during that phase I didn't have the data I needed and, to be honest, I had no idea what it would take to win. Actually, such a plan is no different than many such plans that I had prepared during my business career. Writing competitive proposals to win government contracts often entails several hundred thousand dollars in Bid and Proposal (B&P) costs against your overhead budget. To get approval to spend that kind of money always requires a written assessment of the company's chances of success.

When I worked for Tracor, we had a significant B&P budget, but there were also over a half dozen managers competing for those dollars in order to be able to write proposals to increase their department's business base. I always watched in amusement while the other managers squabbled over what was left in the budget, while I was spending mine *and* their shares writing proposals, having submitted a cohesive capture plan that had been approved and funded. They never seemed to catch on. A political campaign should be approached in much the same manner.

First of all, a well thought out plan will tell you where to focus your energy, and *focus* is the operative word. Secondly, major potential contributors are going to want to see your campaign plan before committing a large contribution. Basically, the plan had two main elements: the numbers, and what made this election different than the last election.

Beverly Kennedy ran against Deutsch in the 1994 election and she got 39% of the vote, losing by a 28,000 vote margin. Starting with this, I surmised that I needed to hold what she had earned, and pick up 15,000 votes that she didn't get and that Deutsch had. Holding what she got would not be a snap, because she had also run against Deutsch in 1992, had good name recognition as a talk show host, and had some political base.

The things that made this election different than the last election was the fact that 1) there was a major issue in the Keys with the Marine Sanctuary that was guaranteed to bring out the vote, 2) I was a veteran, and a veteran had not run in the last two elections in my district, and 3) there had been a surge in Independent voter registration in West Broward since the last election. Ross Perot would probably be on the ballot, with no Reform Party congressional candidate, and I was going to sound a lot like Perot and I thought I could get those votes.

I figured that if I could take 65% of the vote in the Keys, pick up an extra 6500 veterans' votes, and take 65% of the Independent vote, I would have the additional 15000 votes I needed to win.

I fleshed the plan out over four or five pages and shopped it around to the Republican leadership. All agreed that it was a great plan, but a good plan's success lies in its execution, and this plan just never got fully executed. The reason was pure and simple; *time and staff.* I just didn't have the time to get it fully implemented, or the staff to make up for the lack of time.

Another thing that I did during this period was to have myself invited up to the U.S. Sugar Corporation, in Clewiston, Florida (Big Sugar). One of the most emotionally charged referendums on all the ballots in Florida was the one calling for a penny per pound tax on all raw sugar produced to pay for the Everglades clean-up. It was a big issue statewide, but it was a very big issue in South Florida. Mark Foley, the Republican incumbent, whose district actually includes the sugar farms, arranged for my visit, and Ed Clausner and I accepted the invitation.

First of all, one must understand that the character of the Everglades has changed in the past thirty years. The "river of grass" has altered course, and the water that flows through the Everglades from north to south has changed course. As an engineer, my initial reaction was, "So what?" Nor is the sugar industry responsible for this. In 1965, Congress told the U.S. Army Corps of Engineers to "dry out" West Broward, West Dade, and West Palm Beach Counties so that development could take place out to the levees. The Corps did this, and they did a fine job by installing a series of west to east canals as well as a very sophisticated pumping system. These counties are as dry as a bone, and development has occurred to the point that all three counties are almost built out.

Furthermore, the sugar industry was being accused of dumping large amounts of nutrients, including phosphorous, into the Everglades. Bob Coker, the V.P. for Community and Government Affairs, and our host, readily admitted that at one time they had been guilty of this, but no longer. In fact, he showed us proof that the sugar industry was considerably ahead of the schedule imposed upon them by the Everglades Forever Act in reducing this run-off. This fact has also been reported in the media. Published reports by state scientists have reported and published the same findings. So why all the hysteria?

Well, everyone wants to "Save the Everglades", myself included. It is vital to South Florida and it houses our entire water supply. However, as an engineer, I am at least mildly interested in just what it is that we are saving it from, and is the sugar industry really the culprit? I never received a satisfactory answer to the former, but I did find satisfactory answers to the latter in a number of independent studies that seemed to absolve the sugar industry. However, hard facts do little to deter Al Gore and his jolly band of eco-terrorists, who seem to migrate to the warm climates in their never-ending quest for causes. They just took their standard ready-fire-aim approach at the deepest pockets around, belonging to "Big Sugar". Paying a dollar per signature to little old ladies in tennis shoes to hang around the posts offices and shopping malls all over Florida, they managed to collect enough signatures to get the issue on the ballot in every county in Florida.

My exhaustive study of the issue convinced me that the sugar industry was facing a bum rap for a number of reasons. First of all, sugar farming is an environmental-friendly farming process. The nutrients contained in the fertilizers used in sugar farming are quite low in phosphorus, and the sugar plant itself consumes most of what is there, leaving only traces of the phosphorus to return to the soil for potential run-off. Cow turds, on the other hand, are extremely high in phosphorous, and cow turds don't consume shit, so to speak; a profound bit of agri-chemical reality that the environmental community should be able to sink their teeth into. Furthermore there is an abundance of dairy farms in the area that I would call highly suspect. However, the dairy indus-try has nowhere near the deep pockets enjoyed by Big Sugar. Neverthe-less, putting my instinct for political survival ahead of an engineering sagacity peculiar to political circles, I decided that I had best try to stay out of the fray.

Congressman Foley, to the north, has 60,000 sugar jobs to worry about. He is very involved in the issue, as well he should be. However, there are no directly sugar-related jobs in my district, and any support I gave them would probably cost me votes. By the same token, I was not going to support the sugar tax, either, because I felt it was unjustified. It was not a big issue in my campaign, and when it did come up, my position was that I was against the tax because it only caused Big Sugar to pay for part of the cleanup. If they were guilty, they should be charged with pollution, taken to court, and if proven guilty, they should pay for *all* the clean up. This would never happen because they could never be found guilty in a court of law because, in my opinion, they were *not* guilty and the facts overwhelmingly supported that. This is as close as I came to straddling an issue, but I watched Bob Wexler, who won the open seat in District 19 take thousands of dollars of Big Sugar money, and then strongly back the sugar tax. It goes without say-ing that Wexler is a Democrat.

6

POST PRIMARY—THE RACE IS REALLY ON

O nce the primary elections were out of the way, the pace picked up noticeably. Everyone wanted a piece of the candidates' time, including those organizations that would hand out coveted endorsements. Some of them are important, but I have mixed feelings about others. Perhaps the most important are the endorsements of the major newspapers in the area. I was told early on by people with a lot more political savvy than I had that I would never get the endorsement of the Fort Lauderdale Sun-Sentinel or the Miami Herald because I was a Republican candidate, and both papers are liberal leaning. Well, *most* major newspapers, other than the Washington Times, are probably a little left of center. I failed to get either endorsement, but I think I was treated fairly.

First of all, the editorial boards are politically astute, their questions are good questions, and I knew they had read and studied the data I had sent them because it was sometimes reflected in their questions. Kingsley Guy, the Editorial Page Editor and James Driscoll, the Political Editor of the Sun-Sentinel, and Jim Hampton and the Editorial Staff of the Miami Herald interviewed me. I walked away from both interviews feeling that I had given a good accounting of myself, and I actually thought I had a shot at the endorsement. Even recounting my responses while driving home, I couldn't think of an answer I would have changed. Both Editorial Boards interview *every* candidate in *every* race, which I think I read comes to about 300 interviews per year; no small feat. If I could make but one suggestion, I would recommend that they give congressional candidates more than 30 minutes, because the national issues are many and many are complex.

Furthermore, I think it is very difficult for a challenger to receive an endorsement from a major newspaper unless the incumbent has screwed up somewhere along the line. In other words, if the interviews are close, the incumbent will usually get the nod unless there is a compelling reason to withhold it. I happen to agree with that philosophy.

What I thought was unique in my encounter with both papers, and especially with the Key West Citizen, whose endorsement I also failed to receive, is this: Usually, the "losing" candidate is not even mentioned, other than by name, in the endorsement article. I felt all three of these papers went out of their way to say something positive about me, and I did not see this with any other race. I am including their comments below:

Ft. Lauderdale Sun Sentinel—10/15/96

"Jacobs has extensive business experience in other parts of the world at technical and senior management levels for large corporations. He has spent many years working overseas, mainly in Asia and the Middle East, and has thoughtful observations about foreign trade and international relations. The Republican Party, nationally and in Florida, ought to make good use of his expertise and background.

Key West Citizen—10/27/96

"Jacobs is an amiable, decent, eloquent man who speaks sound sense on many issues facing the country today.
He argues for restoration of cuts in the military, calls for an amendment to the U.S. Constitution to require a balanced federal budget, and demands action on making Medicare and Social Security solvent.
He says he opposes the Florida Keys National Marine Sanctuary for fear of what it might mean in excess bureaucracy and govern-

ment interference in individual lives.
If he is elected, Jacobs pledges himself to six years in office only—in
the true tradition of the citizen politician.
We believe either man would serve this district well.

Miami Herald—10/27/96

"Incumbent Peter Deutsch, 39, faces Republican opposition from
Jim Jacobs, 61, a marine consultant, making his first bid for pub-
lic office. Mr. Jacobs is a serious, thoughtful candidate who's also
poorly financed."

Yes, I would like to have received these endorsements, because the papers also print a "tear out" voter's guide on Election Day, and I'm sure a lot of these guides find their way into the voting booths. But, I reiterate, I think I was treated fairly.

Actually, I'm glad I feel this way. The last thing any candidate needs to do it to get crossways with an organization that buys its paper by the ton and its ink by the barrel.

One endorsement interview in which I was *not* treated fairly was with the Greater Ft. Lauderdale Area Realtors. First of all, I have an active real estate salesperson license and I am a licensed real estate mortgage broker. We have all been to interviews or have taken tests where, when we walked out, we knew we had aced it. The recommendation committee consisted of seven people, I believe, and they all gave me a standing ovation as I left. Furthermore, they were concerned about property rights issues, and I nailed every question. A reduction in the capital gains tax came up, and I told them I didn't think it should be reduced, I thought it should be abolished entirely. Conversely, Peter Deutsch has a dismal record on votes involving property rights, and he is a tax maven. Frankly, I was shocked when I did not receive their endorsement. I was told later by someone who was not on the committee, but who was in a position to know, that I received the unanimous recommendation of the committee, but that the Board of

Realtors reversed the recommendation. While this was certainly within their rights, I think it was grossly unfair.

Two other endorsement interviews with which I was less than thrilled concerned both the Broward County and the Dade County Police Benevolent Associations. Both are unions, and in this election, with national unions spending millions of dollars in absolutely illegal contributions to unseat Republican sitting Members, union leaderships were not going to endorse very many Republicans. The reason for this is that the Republican Party is committed to downsizing the federal government. Thirty-eight percent of the employees of the federal government belong to unions, as opposed to 14% of the workers in the private sector. However, with this particular union, their big issue seemed to be my stand on gun control and my stand on the assault weapons ban. Of course, I support the ban on *automatic* weapons, and this restriction was passed as the National Firearms Act in 1935. The "assault weapons ban" restricts weapons that are nothing more than semi-automatic long rifles with perfectly legitimate hunting and sporting applications. I am also a strong supporter on the Second Amendmen that gives citizens the right to bear arms. Most police on the streets support having an armed citizenry of law-abiding gun owners, and most recognize that, since the Right to Carry law was passed in Florida in 1987, homicide by handgun is down 38%, while it is up an average of over 20% in states with strict gun control laws. In fact, following a debate in the Keys in which Deutsch tried to set me up with a question on the Automatic Weapons Ban, I had a Federal Marshall follow me out of the hall and tell me that he fully supported my position on the issue.

During this phase of the campaign cycle, the candidate forums began to pick up in frequency with sometimes two or three forums scheduled in one evening. The Public TV debates were also coming up.

One station, WPBT-TV in West Palm Beach, had scheduled a debate for all of the congressional nominees in the five active races. In two of the districts in Dade County, both Republican incumbents were running unopposed, Ileana Ros-Lehtinen and Lincoln Diaz-Bal-art. This debate had been scheduled for quite some time and, after the paucity of news coverage, I was hungry for some exposure. I was comfortable with my speaking ability and I was certainly comfortable with the issues. I had endured enough forum exposure to iron the kinks out of my lines, and I knew what worked for me, and what didn't. I also had a few well-practiced "sound bites". These are statements that are carefully word-smithed to make it onto the eleven o'clock news. An interview with a TV reporter might last anywhere from 30 seconds to a minute, but only one or two sentences will get quoted on the air. The trick is to make sure what does get on the air is what you *want* to be on the air.

About three weeks before this first TV debate, the station called and apologetically explained that they had to drop my race. When I asked the reason, they explained that the time allotted, and the format planned could not support five races. They felt they should drop our race, since this district didn't include Palm Beach County. Well, their Palm Beach County TV transmitter sure as hell reached our district. I was quite disappointed because I really needed the exposure.

A week or so later, a representative from the American Association of Retired People (AARP) called and canceled another debate that was to have included all the congressional candidates and which was to have been taped live in front of an audience of about 500 people. The reason, she said, was they were unable to get the commitment of some of the incumbents, so they decided to cancel the whole thing. Unhappy though I was, I still had not put all of this together.

After the first debate was held and aired without me or Peter, Steve Bosquet, the political writer for the Miami Herald, reported on the debate in his column. He included the statement that neither Peter Deutsch nor Jim Jacobs had been available for the debate. Not available, my ass. I went ballistic.

I called the station and demanded an explanation. After some hemming and hawing, they finally admitted that the reason they dropped my race was, indeed, because Deutsch cited other commitments and would not be able to attend. It was well into September and I had not yet even faced Deutsch. Faced him, hell, I hadn't even met him. It suddenly became clear that he was ducking me. I called the political desks of both the Sun-Sentinel and the Herald and made that charge. Both Bosquet and Buddy Nivens, the political columnist for the Sun-Sentinel, seemed to be quite interested in this fact. As far as I know, that is the last time he actually pulled this. I can only surmise that both may have whispered in Deutsch's ear.

Actually, we had both *seemed* to appear on one TV debate, but we had not appeared together. This was on WXEL-TV in Delray Beach, in which all the candidates were scheduled for taping at different times. The tapes were then put together and edited to make it appear that we had actually been facing each other on the same stage. This taping session was almost a disaster. It was scheduled fairly early in the morning about an hour's drive away. I'm not a morning person anyway, and I managed to get lost trying to find the place. We barely made the time they had scheduled, and the hostess did little to make me feel comfortable. Usually there is a little warm-up, but she got right to it. I asked about re-takes and was told that it would have to be a pretty bad screwup to warrant a re-take.

The questions had been pre-taped and the first one flashed on the monitor in front of me. The president of a local Chamber of Commerce posed it and it had to do with Affirmative Action. Well, I'm not a big fan of the Affirmative Action Program, and I knew that he must be or he wouldn't have posed the subject as his question. Of course, I had an answer, but it wasn't the answer that I'm sure a lot of his audience would want to hear. I have been dealing with Affirmative Action since its inception. As with all government programs designed to correct an ill, the solution usually over-corrects and creates other ills. This is especially true of the provision in the law known as '8-A'. This provision allows for certain government competitive procurements to be set aside for minority firms. For every legitimate '8-A' firm, there are a dozen that are operated essentially as "fronts". Having secured a government contract under this ruse, the '8-A' company will turn around and subcontract most of the work to a company that was locked out of competing on the procurement in the first place. This results in millions, if not billions of dollars in added costs to the government. While I certainly believe that all companies should be guaranteed an opportunity, I don't think any company should be guaranteed an outcome.

Actually, you don't always get the questions you would like to answer. But combined with everything else, plus the fact that this was my first TV appearance, I walked out of there thinking I had really bombed.

I never knew when these programs were going to air, and I didn't have time to watch TV anyhow. A couple of weeks later, a friend called me at home and said that the debate was being aired right then, and gave me the channel number. I managed to catch it and it wasn't nearly as bad as I had thought it would be. This was also the first time I had seen Deutsch on TV, and Peter wasn't that great, either. A few nights later, unable to sleep, I was channel surfing late at night and I came across it on a Spanish station *in Spanish*. Actually, I think I liked the Spanish version better.

When I tell you I didn't have time for TV, I am serious. There was usually something scheduled every night. I don't like to eat early, so we never had dinner before we went to whatever function was scheduled. We tried to have dinner during the 11 o'clock news, and I usually fell asleep watching "Nightline".

During one three day, two night trip to the Keys for a number of forums, we stayed in Marathon, about half way down the Keys. On the first night we had a big forum in Key West, and the next night in Big Pine Key. We didn't get out of the Key West forum until almost one o'clock, and by the time we got back to Marathon it was after two. The only thing open was a "Denny's". The next night it was more of the same. Thank God for Denny's or we would have starved to death.

Speaking of getting lost on the way to the WXEL taping, it seemed like I *stayed* lost throughout most of the campaign. I have an uncanny sense of direction, but that is of little value if you don't know where you are going in the first place. This is another thing that was stressed in candidate school. A cardinal rule is to insure that your driver knows where he is going. The NRCC even suggests that the driver make a practice run in many cases. Well, I very rarely had a driver and God forbid I would ever do something sensible like putting a map in the car. I conservatively estimate that I was lost a cumulative of twelve hours during a four-month period.

The Florida Republican Party gave one of the best tools that I had in this entire campaign to me. It is a database program called "Victory Suite". That first time I spoke with Bev Kennedy, when she told me what great legs she had, she also offered to sell me her data base of the 20th Congressional District for $50,000. Here I am running on my astute business acumen and I'm going to pay that kind of money for a database; especially from *someone who lost with it?* I don't think so. Besides, when we were at Presidency III, I had been introduced to Scott McPherson, a paid staffer at the Florida Republican Party headquarters in Tallahassee, who was reportedly putting together the end-all in political databases to be used by the various Republican County Executive Committees. Scott describes himself as a "computer weenie with an attitude". The program was not complete when I saw it, but I immediately recognized that it would be an important campaign tool.

When I went to campaign school shortly after Presidency III, various vendors of campaign aids were also peripherally present. There was one company present, Aristotle, who had a mobile van set-up outside the hotel where the school was being held. They offered a number of campaign databases, but they were not cheap, far outside my projected budget. Anyhow, being fairly computer literate, I could see the advantage of having such a tool at my disposal.

"Victory Suite" was made available to me through the Republican Party. Since 75% of my district was in Broward County, the Broward portion was made available. There are approximately 800,000 registered voters in Broward County, 300,000 of which are in District 20. Accordingly, I had to load the entire 800,000-person database onto my computer just to get at the 202 precincts in my district. I was under the impression that I had pretty much of an ass-kicking computer, but with what I already had on it, it wouldn't take this program. So, right in the middle of the heat of battle, I had to dismantle the whole computer configuration and take my CPU in and add a new 1.2 gig harddrive. I had already loaded the Monroe County database, courtesy of Harry Sawyer, the Monroe County Supervisor of Elections, and all I was lacking were the thirty-nine Dade County precincts.

Getting these turned out to be a trip through Wonderland. The people at the Dade County Elections Office were cooperative enough, but the only formats they offered were a mainframe tape of the database, a list, or labels. I chose the mainframe tape and took it to a company who could convert it to discs that I could insert into my computer, only to learn that something else had to be done, etc., etc. I have a fairly short attention span, especially when the creek is backing up. It wasn't that this database wasn't important; it just became *too hard*.

"Victory Suite" allows one to do almost anything in the manipulation of voters lists, from generating mailing lists by precinct, to pulling up demographics by precinct, to generating walking lists, listing each household member on a given street complete with their voting history and party affiliation, you name it. One can even tie it into the mail-merge capability on the word processor and address personal letters and envelopes to every voter in a particular precinct. It was when I was being phone-walked through this procedure late one night by one of Scott's staffers, a *very* patient gentleman named Malcomb Meekison, that he remarked, "You know, you are working with the Broward

County data-base. What you really need is the 20th Congressional District database." *Say, what??*

Fortunately, he was quick to add that this didn't exist yet, although it did exist for some congressional districts in Florida. I am sure this tool will be put in place in its finished form during the next election cycle, and should I decide to try this again, it will be one of the cornerstones of my campaign. For this and other reasons, I think we have a great State Republican Party machine. I can't say the same for Broward County.

Not being a politician, I was understandably ignorant of the local political process, starting with the fact that I got lost trying to find the Broward County executive party headquarters when I made my first foray into the political arena. However, I *am* a fairly quick study. The purpose of the Broward County Executive Committee (BREC), is to staff county precincts with "Committee-people", ideally one "Committeeman" and one "Committeewoman" in each precinct in the respective county. The reason they do this is so that any candidate who chooses to put themselves through the gauntlet of running for office has an in-place organization dedicated to helping them get elected by working at the grassroots level. This is what is called the "political machine". These organizations are not funded by the national or state political organizations, but rather by local political fund-raising efforts. Their sole purpose in life is to *get Republican candidates elected to office.*

The meeting that I drove back from the Keys to attend was my first brush with the membership of this executive committee. As I have already mentioned, Jeb Bush was the speaker that evening. Jeb Bush lost the election in 1994 trying to unseat Lawton Chiles, the Governor of the State of Florida. Broward County essentially cost him the race. Introducing him that night was Lew Keller, the Broward County Chairman of this committee. Lew was appropriately contrite in his opening remarks in introducing Jeb, in that he admitted Broward County's culpability in that election. His theme was, "Never Again". Well, it takes more than rhetoric, because it did happen again.

Broward County had a full slate of very well qualified candidates in this election. Of the eighteen candidates on the ballot, *two* were elected; Clay Shaw, the seven term Republican Congressman, who is usually unopposed, and who faced a very weak candidate, and Jane Carroll, the Supervisor of Elections for the past eighteen years, who is also usually unopposed. She won in a very close race. All this was in an election cycle when the Democratic Executive Committee should have been on its ass because *their* Chairman had just been convicted and sentenced to prison on tax charges. The difference was that they still did their job and BREC fell on their sword.

I have 202 precincts in Broward County in my congressional district, and 97 precincts were without the representation of either a committeeman or a committeewoman. In other words, in half of my districts, I had no representation whatsoever. It was essentially the same countywide. In half of the precincts, the Republican slate of candidates had no precinct representation. What is even more appalling, since 1994, when the Democrats handed us Jeb Bush's head, only twenty-four committeepersons were recruited and installed in the precincts making up my district in Broward County.

I assure you, I could sit down at the telephone, and in two months I could contact, interview, and either appoint, or bring to a ballot enough qualified and motivated candidates to fill these ranks, given the authority.

The reason for this debacle was that Chairman Lew Keller was retiring, and the fight over who was to replace him in December took a massive priority at the expense of all of the candidates whose elections were in November. We have met the enemy, and it is *us*.

I want to make a distinction here between the Executive Committee as an entity, and many of the individuals that are members of that committee, the precinct captains. There were precinct captains who took responsibility for three or four precincts, in addition to the one they were assigned, trying to take up the slack for those precincts that were unmanned, or whose occupant's attention was otherwise diverted.

Rich Ramos, the Executive Director of this committee, Barbara Collier, and Kevin Tyner did everything they possibly could to help my campaign. Will Connelly, the Editor of the BREC newsletter, gave me more than my share of space in the Republican Newsletter, and there were many others. But as a political machine, we slung a rod.

Without a doubt, the biggest bloc of support that I *did* get in this campaign came from *members* of the National Rifle Association (NRA). Just as in the paragraph above, I want to draw a clear distinction between these members and the NRA itself. It was also through the NRA that I picked up some more "eagles". Al Hanson is a Dade County Committeeman, and his precinct isn't even in my district. Nevertheless, Al recruited other "eagles", such as Mike Padikulis and Bob Ashton, Homestead gun-owners and avid hunters, who worked tirelessly in my behalf building and putting up signs in South Dade.

Al can probably out-talk Joe Bell and, just as Joe knows everyone worth knowing in the Upper Keys, Al knows everyone worth knowing in South Dade. It was exactly as I had told Sandy; the people that were really helping us, we had never even met before this campaign. Al hosted a Wednesday night strategy session at his house almost every week, and whatever I got in Dade County, I probably got through the efforts of those Wednesday night "eagles".

I guess I attracted this support from my stand on gun control. First of all, as mentioned earlier, I am a strong supporter of the Second Amendment that gives the citizens the right to bear arms, *right* being the operative word. There are those out there who are working overtime to take away this right; Jim Brady and his wife leading the charge. I have met Jim Brady, and what happened to him is a national tragedy. But he is wrong! Furthermore, the Brady Bill has done nothing, nor will it ever do anything to get guns off the streets. Criminals bent on obtaining a handgun do not walk into the local gun shop and buy one, as do law-abiding citizens. For the record, I, too, am for getting guns off the street. However, where I split the blanket with the anti-gun bleeding hearts is that I am for getting guns *into the home.*

One only needs to look at our nation's capital, Washington, D.C., to see the futility of gun control laws. Washington, D.C. has probably the strictest gun control laws in the entire country. It is absolutely illegal to own a handgun, period. You cannot even keep a handgun in your house. Yet, Washington has the highest crime and homicide rate in the nation. Other facts and statistics are just as compelling, with the states having liberal gun laws, and especially liberal right-to-carry laws, being much less prone to violent crime.

These are the facts that I look at in putting forth my hard stand against gun control. We are all born with certain unrestricted rights, the right granted under the Second Amendment being one of them. Sometimes we vote to give up these rights, usually to keep peace or for the common good. Until such time as I become convinced that giving up this particular right will keep the peace, or result in a common good, I will steadfastly maintain my view on gun control.

The assault weapon issue is just another way the liberals have at chipping away at this right. Certainly, I do not believe that our citizens should be running around with automatic weapons, but the assault weapons ban is not about automatic weapons. The National Firearms Act of 1935 keeps these automatic weapons out of the hands of unregistered individuals. I fully support the provisions of that Act. Again, assault weapons, as defined under the Assault Weapons Ban, include semi-automatic long rifles that have very legitimate hunting and sporting applications. The argument I kept hearing, especially from the Police Benevolent Associations, was that one could modify these weapons and make them fully automatic. That is true, but then the weapon becomes illegal under the National Firearms Act, rendering the Assault Weapons ban clearly restrictive on law-abiding citizens engaging in legal hunting and sporting pursuits, and redundant once these weapons might become modified.

My opponent wants to completely disarm everyone. His sole argument is that guns kill people. My argument is that *people kill people*. During several of our debates, the format allowed for each to ask the other a "hard" question. I had a whole pocketful for Peter, but he just kept serving up the assault weapon issue, and I just kept hitting it out of the park. I dropped the line on him several times that if he had founded Mothers Against Drunk Drivers (MADD), he would have called it "Mothers Against Cars". Peter has a slow learning curve.

In spite of all of this, I never got a dime of PAC money out of the NRA, even though they gave me an 'A' rating in their nationally published voters guide. The way PACs work was explained to us in candidate school and, like everything else that the NRCC put out at the school, this was borne out in practice. PACs have just so much money to dispense. Approximately 80% of it goes to incumbents, because 90% of incumbents win re-election. Furthermore, those individuals who make the decisions on who gets contributions are "graded" on how many winners they backed during an election cycle. I'm sure there is a small amount of money set aside to "buy insurance" by backing a challenger if it looks like he, or she, might have a chance to oust an enemy incumbent. However, in most situations these PAC decision-makers rely heavily on polls from reputable polling organizations. These polls cost a lot of money. Thus, it becomes a pretty vicious circle. Those candidates, who need the money the most to possibly unseat a candidate undesirable to that particular PAC, don't have the money to spend on polling data, which is a requirement for making your case to the PAC to obtain money to be used in unseating that undesirable candidate. If that last thought is a little too profound, read it again. Joseph Heller made a fortune with this concept. He called it *Catch 22*!

Furthermore, PACs *never* dispense money to a challenger until after the primaries. I wasted a lot of time and effort trying to get money from several PACs that I felt I could honestly support after the primaries had been decided. I had picked up a good following of NRA members in the Keys and in South Dade, including the NRA District Coordinator, Jim Janda. I know Jim and other active members wrote letters, and made calls to the NRA headquarters on my behalf, all to no avail.

It was also about this time, just before the final month of the campaign, that I finally resigned myself to the fact that this campaign just was not going to have a campaign manager. I had interviewed a number of prospective campaign managers in Washington, when I was still testing the waters, but found no one with whom I was particularly comfortable. One young man that I interviewed in Washington had impeccable credentials in other campaigns in senior positions, although he had never actually managed a campaign. He was a Marine Corps veteran and he wanted to move to South Florida because his fiancee lived in Boca Raton. We hit it off well, but there was a hooker.

He confided that he had been adopted, and because of this, he could not be comfortable with my stand on abortion. Doesn't it ever end? He felt that had his birth mother shared my belief, he would not be around. That's not necessarily true, but I have already belabored that point. We met again in Florida, once I was a candidate, and talked about it again. I really think he wanted to come aboard, and I think I had succeeded in making my point about *my* stand on the issue, but he had also been offered a much better paying job with Blockbuster Entertainment, which he decided to take. He made the right decision, and at least he made it for the right reason.

After my hat was in the ring, I was always on the lookout for someone to manage the campaign for me. Nobody knew I needed such a person more than I did. However, there was always the question of how I was going to pay this person. I finally found myself at the point of realizing that, even if I found somebody who would work for free, or relatively cheaply, I didn't even have the time to bring them up to speed. I decided that I had gotten that far without a campaign manager, so I might as well hit the home-stretch without one. I put it out of my mind.

I had put the idea of hiring a political consultant out of my mind a long time ago, partly because of the money problem, but also because I couldn't quite figure out what it was that they do. I was pretty comfortable with my own political instincts, which, in retrospect, were not all that bad. I also kept watching Bob Dole stumble on an almost daily basis and he had some of the best political consultants in the country. And, as Sandy remarked one day, it wouldn't matter who I had as a consultant; if it came down to a conflict, I would do what I wanted to do anyway. She was probably right. Yeah, Dick Morris undoubtedly gave Clinton the winning strategy, but I am of the opinion that a candidate for national office should set his own political agenda, based on what he *believes*, rather that that which is crafted by a hired gun aimed at the gut of the voter. Furthermore, if a candidate is not able to accomplish that on his own, perhaps he should seek another line of work. On the other hand, here is a loser trying to tell a bunch of winners how to play the game. Well, it *is my book.*

With those nagging decisions out of the way, I was ready for the final mile to the election.

7

THE LAST MILE

The run-off elections were finally held in District 19, to the north, and the press suddenly realized that there were other races and other candidates out there. A couple of fairly significant TV debates were scheduled and some of the larger and more meaningful candidate forums were forthcoming. The National Republican Party (NRC) opened a "Victory '96" Dole Campaign party headquarters, plus two satellite offices in Broward County, one of which was in the middle of my district. This office was essentially taken over by the Southwest Broward Republican Club, of which I was a member. The club had several candidates that had survived the primaries and the General Election slate was finally complete.

Officially, this satellite office was my campaign office, but all of the candidates used it, more or less, for a gathering place. My computer was at home, and I spent a lot of time on the computer. Basically, I ran this campaign from my home, encroaching more and more on our available domestic space until Sandy was about ready to move into campaign headquarters just to get away from it.

Serious campaigning kicked in literally overnight. Phone banks were established at the "Victory '96" Headquarters, mail-outs were going to all the requesters of absentee ballots, and volunteers were signing up for a myriad of tasks now that it began to dawn on the masses that there was about to be an election.

Let me say a word about absentee ballots. Any time one is out campaigning, the candidate never knows whether or not whoever is being addressed is even a registered voter, much less whether that person might actually make it to the polls. However, voters who go to the trouble to request an absentee ballot almost always vote. All campaign organizations treat these potential voters very seriously and immediately mail campaign materials for their candidates to these requesters, usually right on the heels of the ballot itself. In fact, in Key West our volunteers were picking up the absentee requests on a daily basis and getting campaign literature into the mail the following day to those absentee voters.

The major newspapers even awoke to the fact that there were races other than the District 19 race and the school board race. The Miami Herald assigned a reporter full time to this race, a young, very capable reporter named Meg James. Meg called me and explained her assignment, and I suggested we meet for lunch. I like to get to know the people with whom I am dealing, and I felt she could do a better job of reporting if she knew more about me and about where I was coming from. Maybe I am still naive, but I think covering a campaign is a two-way street. Reporters have their job to do and their deadlines to meet, and let's face it, they can make you or break you. I am convinced that the reason I feel I was fairly treated by the press is because I treated them with respect. Meg did a lot of probing, and I was straight up with her. She even picked up the lunch check. The girl will go far.

All of this was coming down and *I still had not met Peter Deutsch*. I was about ready to have his picture put on milk cartons to see if anyone had seen him.

This finally changed the evening of October 7th at a candidate forum sponsored by a homeowner's group, The Driftwood Civic Association in Hollywood, less than a dozen blocks from where Deutsch made his home. Actually, I had had a schedule conflict, and had not planned to be at this forum. My conflict was resolved during that afternoon, so I decided to attend the Driftwood meeting. I strongly suspect that Peter knew that I would not be there and accordingly, decided to show up. I think he was about as surprised to see me, as I was to see him. He was cordial and surprisingly gracious. So was I.

Peter asked the moderator if he could go on first, as he had another commitment; a line I would become very accustomed to hearing. What the hell, it got me on second, and more important, out of there ahead of about a dozen other candidates for other races, who were waiting to speak. This was the first time I had seen him "live".

Frankly, for a 14-year seasoned politician, I did not think he was all that polished a speaker. He said his piece and left with his aide, whom I don't think ever left his side during the last month of the campaign. He didn't even stick around for my presentation, for which this same aide later apologized. It was just as well. This turned out to be one of those "dream forums", where the questions from the floor just kept coming. This was my element; mike in hand, no podium, a neutral audience, and lots of questions. I must have been up there for a good forty-five minutes, an occurrence almost unheard of with several other candidates awaiting their turn. However, in spite of a lot of candidates looking at their watches, I wasn't about to relinquish the mike until the moderator took it, and it took him a long time to do so. Usually, having three minutes to make my case and being limited to one, or maybe two questions, getting this sort of reception and interest had me leaving there walking on air.

The next night there was a TV debate sponsored by the Greater Plantation Chamber of Commerce, and Peter was again up to his old tricks. He sent his head spear-chucker, Henry Ellen-Bogen. Henry is a nice enough guy, but I was getting kind of tired of debating him instead of Deutsch. I never did really figure out Peter's strategy, if indeed, he even had one. But, I think that if voters go to the trouble of attending one of these forums, they have the right to expect to see and hear from the candidate, rather than a surrogate. The only other thing scheduled that night, of which I was aware, was a "Friends of the NRA" dinner in Key Biscayne. I hardly think Peter was at that.

This particular forum wasn't one of my better performances. We were scheduled late in the program, and some of the candidates that I had let cool it the evening before took their pound of flesh and started filing out just as we were introduced.

Furthermore, we were seated, which I don't like, but most annoying was the TV cameraman. He must have been a liberal because he had a habit of shaking his head every time I said something with which he didn't agree, which was essentially everything I had to say. It was impossible to ignore him because I had to look right at him. I guess that's show biz.

When the tape aired, I felt that, again, I came off better than I thought I had. I also met Alcee Hastings for the first time, as he followed Henry and me, and we had a chance to chat in the hall. He was a federal judge that was impeached by Congress earlier, and who engineered a comeback by getting elected to Congress and subsequently winning the respect of many of those Members of Congress who had voted for his impeachment.

Hastings is one of our more liberal Democratic representatives, and I certainly don't agree with his politics, but I liked the man immediately.

It was also getting to be time to start thinking about TV ads. I had pretty much assumed that I wouldn't be able to buy any TV time, for lack of money, but a spate of contributions started coming in; spate, to me being nickels and dimes to anyone else. I also made the decision that every dime that I received between then and the election would be used to buy TV time. All our bills were paid, our signage was bought, we had enough campaign literature to get through the election, and we even had a couple of thousand in the bank. Like everything else that I faced in this campaign, I didn't know a damn thing about buying TV time.

Actually, federal election law has taken much of the mystery out of it. The networks and the cable providers are required to give all candidates their lowest rates and, short of being sold out, they are required to make TV time available to all candidates. Nat Treger, the talk show host with whom I had made my radio debut, had urged me to block out some time before all the choice channels were sold out. He also agreed to help me put together the commercials, since I had never done that, either. I had to limit myself to cable TV because broadcast TV was just too expensive. The other problem with broadcast TV was that, because of the population density of South Florida, with a third of the population of the entire state concentrated in one broadcast market, every commercial hit eight congressional districts. This meant that less than 15% of those that saw one of my commercials could actually vote for me. With this type of media demographics, and the resultant cost thereof, I decided that cable TV would be my designated medium.

With cable TV, I could target only my district, but I still had to deal with five different cable companies; four in Broward County and one in the Keys. To get started, I just picked up the phone and started calling them all, setting up appointments with their sales reps, all of who were bright, sharp, young women. On each cable network channel, thirty second spots cost anywhere from $7 to $10 each between 6 am and 12 PM. Prime time "guarantees" run about double that, although some of the former find their way into prime time just on normal rotation. On the other hand, broadcast TV, such as ABC, CBS, and NBC, cost about $1000 per pop, definitely a no-brainer in my limited financial circumstances.

Lacking a better reference, I stuck pretty close to cable CNN and Headline News because that is what I watch most often. A $50,000 political consultant could probably have helped me with this. Nevertheless, I think I got a lot of bang-for-the-buck. A couple of my commercials even hit the *Larry King Live* time slot on CNN.

Somebody, somewhere, told me that each 30-second spot on cable TV will be seen by 300 people on average. Since I was only able to spend $5000 on TV, and bought about 600 spots, using this formula indicates that 180,000 viewers saw at least one of my ads. Even that sounds overly optimistic to me, but a blitz it wasn't. With 400,000 voters, theoretically I hit only half of them *one time*. Well, I'm sure no one could complain about getting sick of seeing my face on the tube.

Another thing I found out about buying TV time was that you pay up front. This really was not a hindrance, because with my austere budget, we had been paying cash up front for everything. I also learned that the stations needed anywhere from a day and a half to four days to make changes when you wanted to make a change in your commercial, or substitute commercials, depending on when they made their "insertions". Automation is wonderful.

Having blocked out some time, the next step was to think about getting the commercials actually made, and "in the can", suitable for handing over to the cable TV channels, along with my check, of course.

In the work ethic that I have developed over the past forty-plus years, I have always felt that if what you are doing isn't fun, it becomes *work*. Nobody really likes to *work*. I looked at writing, and essentially producing these commercials as being fun. I think a couple of my commercials were great, but then, I wrote them. Again, I shopped around. I was planning to make four different commercials; one "positive", you know, "I'm Jim Jacobs. Vote for me because I'm a good guy," and all that. The other three would be "attack" ads; going after Deutsch *on the issues*, not to be confused with a personal attack. I had decided very early on that I was going to run on Deutsch's record.

Deutsch, like most Democrats, goes to Washington and is a liberal for twenty-two months out of each election cycle. Then he comes home and runs for re-election as a conservative. One thing is absolutely consistent with Peter; *he lies*. In the meantime, I had to get the commercials in the can and get them to the various stations because I wanted them to start two weeks before the election. Again, this is too late, but it was the best I could do with what money I had.

Writing the commercials was easy. It took me less than an hour to write the four. As I said, I thought they were great, everybody I showed them to thought they were great, my E-mail filled up with notes saying they were great, people called me and said they were great, and one little old lady called me and asked me how I could say those things about that nice Mr. Deutsch. Well, I guess, even a monkey falls out of the tree every once in awhile.

Having the storyboards in hand, I shopped around for estimates on getting the commercials produced. I received quotes ranging from $10000 each to $500 for all four, the latter bid being from Jones Intercable in Davie, only a couple of miles from my house.

Working with the people at Jones Intercable was one of the bright spots in the entire campaign. From the lady that sold me the airtime, Laura Ewing, to the Production Manager, Frank Bianca, to the very talented young lady that did the production, Jackie Corbiere, I found this organization to be absolutely "top drawer". Laura even took the time to check in with me when we were making the commercials to make sure everything was going to my satisfaction. Of course, I saw a lot of professionally produced political ads on TV during the election, and judging from the estimates I received, I can only imagine what they must have cost to produce. But, when all you're trying to do is shoot the wolves nearest the sled, Jones Intercable came through for me like a Royal Mountie in a snowbank full of dead wolves. They also came through later, as I will get to.

I have just got to comment here on the other end of the spectrum. During the writing of this book, we experienced a thing called the Super Bowl. Much was made of the Super Bowl commercials, which aired at a price of $1.2 *million* for each 30-second spot. I understand reaching an audience. If 100 million people were reached with each ad, the advertisers reached 83 people per dollar spent. Not too much difference than me reaching 300 people with a $10 spot. What I don't understand is the production costs of these spots. It is reported that these ads cost an average of $500,000 each to produce. How in the hell can you spend a half million dollars on a 30 second spot?

Hey, Corporate America! Have I got a deal for you. And, here of late, I happen to have some time available.

I won't put the reader through all of these commercials, but I do want to talk about "The Rattlesnake". You see, it got your attention already.

Deutsch voted with Bill Clinton for the largest tax increase in the history of this country in 1993. This was after Clinton first got elected by promising the American people a tax cut if he was elected. One sound bite that I used effectively in the campaign was, "Bill Clinton said during his 1992 campaign that if we voted for Bush, we would get a tax increase. I voted for Bush, and, sure enough, I got a tax increase."

The insidious part of this particular tax increase, as I saw it, was that it also increased the amount of Social Security income received by senior citizens that was subject to federal income tax from 50% to 85%. This unnecessary tax was levied on the people who could least afford it, the seniors. When the Republican 104th Congress sought to repeal this part of the tax, labeled as the Republican-led Seniors Relief Act, Deutsch voted against that as well. I saw it as a "double whammy" against the very people that sent Deutsch to Congress, the mostly retired condo voters in Broward County. I hammered him on this at every opportunity, and you're probably getting tired of hearing it. I also hammered on it in my commercials.

The storyboard for the "Rattlesnake" ad is as follow:

VIDEO	VOICE OVER
Show picture of a rattlesnake with tail rattling	This is a rattlesnake
Show picture of Peter Deutsch	This is Peter Deutsch. Peter voted to raise the tax on your Social Security Income by 35%. When Republicans tried to repeal that tax, he voted against it.
Show the rattlesnake striking directly at the camera	This snake will bite you.
Show picture of Deutsch	Peter bit you twice.

Jim Jacobs (Live)

(Live) I'm Jim Jacobs, and I hate snakes. I have signed a binding agreement never to vote to raise taxes as long as I am in Congress.

Elect Jim Jacobs and we will lower everyone's taxes, and we will repeal that Social Security tax, and that's a promise.

Jacobs walks off camera, shaking his head   God, I hate snakes!

Remember Indiana Jones in "The Temple of Doom"

My rationale on commercials is the same as it is on my speeches, Ole Blue Eye's song goes, "I've Gotta Be Me". Plus, there are thousands of commercials bombarding the airwaves during the final stages of an election campaign and everybody is beginning to grow sick of them. Starting as late as I did with the commercials, I needed an attention-getter. Rattlesnakes have a way of doing that.

I took this storyboard with me when I went to meet Nat Treger, who was going to help me put some commercials together. He looked at the storyboard and said, "You can't call a U.S. Congressman a snake!"

"I'm not calling him a snake," I said.

"The hell you're not," said he. "You're referring to a United States Congressman as a rattlesnake."

"Godammit, I'm talking about taxes. The snake just happened to be a handy prop," I insisted.

"Well, you're going to really get him pissed off," Nat warned.

"Well, he's already got me pissed off," I came back. "He's been stealing my signs, for christsake!"

And so it went.

He helped me write some good commercials, but it was just like Sandy said; I was going to go with my gut feeling and I really wanted to make, and air, this particular commercial.

Actually, the rattlesnake was not all that handy a prop. I showed up at the Jones Intercable studio with everything but the rattlesnake. Frank Bianca liked the storyboard, but wanted to know where we were going to get the snake. I reminded him that I had done all the creative stuff, like writing the script, producing the storyboard, bringing footage of Deutsch, and showing up with my checkbook. All he had to do was produce the rest of the footage and provide the props, i.e. a rattlesnake, and put it in viewable format.

Frank allowed as how maybe we could borrow a rattlesnake from a local reptile farm, bring it back to the studio, and shoot some footage. I allowed as how that was a great idea, but he could damn well go and get it, and don't forget to yell, "Hey, y'all watch this," when you put it in your car. I might have a *slow* learning curve, but I do have one; I gave up lassoing mailboxes and I lack the faith necessary for snake handling. Besides, such is beyond the job description of a candidate aspiring for national office.

We shot all of the footage for all four commercials that involved me, and copied the footage of Deutsch that I had on tape from one of his ill-fated meetings in Key West. He always seemed to have ill-fated meeting when he went to Key West. Jackie Cobiere, the very talented producer, kept mumbling something while she was editing the footage and voice-overs for the first three commercials to the effect that, "I like these, but I know I'm going to like the rattlesnake best." She even offered me a part-time job writing commercials. I told her that if I didn't win this election, I was probably going to need a full-time job.

The ultimate solution on the logistics involving the rattlesnake proved to be deceptively simple and a hell of a lot less dangerous than Frank's plan. I went to the library and checked out a video tape on reptiles. Copyright attorneys can't be as mean as rattlesnakes.

I called Nat Treger and told him that I had made the "rattlesnake" commercial. I conceded that I knew how he felt about insinuating that a U.S. Congressman might emulate a snake, but that I just wanted him to see it before he passed final judgment. I promised him that I would rely on his judgment. I lied.

Nat viewed the spot and said, "Run it. It's great!"

Narrations and storyboards don't necessarily give the true picture. If the reader is turned off by the preceding narrative, please write me and I will send you a copy of this commercial. If you are still turned off, well, you probably didn't vote for me anyway, and you probably never will.

I was depending on a heavy veteran's vote, that being a key element of my campaign capture plan. However, in retrospect, I never really got the plan off the ground. The main problem was that I waited too late to start, but the reality was that I just didn't have the time or the manpower to get it going. About the only shot that I was able to fire came at an opportunity to address a district meeting of the VFW in Key West during this "last mile". Larry Blocher, my Advisor for Military Affairs, put me in touch with the District Director of the VFW for South Florida, who set it up. The VFW is technically a non-partisan group, but, like any veteran, I think their membership tends to give preference to veterans over non-veterans. I was told in advance that I would not be allowed to give a "campaign speech". I asked if I could just do some Clinton bashing, and was told that, not only was that allowable, but it was encouraged.

Veterans are inherently comfortable around other veterans. This is not something you think about, but subconsciously, you feel a kinship because of the common, and highly personal experience you have shared. I think it places you apart from the crowd.

Of course, I am not a Clinton fan. I think he is unfit to be President of the United States because he is unfit to be the Commander-in-Chief, which is part of the job description. You can watch Clinton when he is around the military and see that he is very uncomfortable. Well he should be. He doesn't understand the military, and he does not have their respect. His policy on gays in the military speaks volumes about his lack of understanding of anything to do with the military.

My feelings on this particular issue are even a little hazy. I have served in the military with gays and I never saw a problem arise from it. To answer the timeworn clique of would I want to share a foxhole with one who is gay, the answer is: I don't care what he is as long as he has a weapon and knows how to use it. Basically, my bottom-line comes down to the "needs of the military". One must remember that serving in the military is not a right; it is a distinct privilege, and the military is anything but a democracy. When a sergeant says to take that hill, you don't stand around and vote on it, you take the goddamn hill. Even the U.S. Supreme Court has historically given wide latitude to the unique needs of the military. Nor can one serve if he is too short, or too tall, or too fat, or has flat feet, or a host of other ailments. In other words, the Pentagon gives the Congress its standards for what kind of men or women it needs to get the job done. Nor is there any place in the military for political correctness, to which I think our more recent military leaders have succumbed with predictably detrimental effects. Just look at the circular firing squads the generals and admirals have convened recently to knock each other off over past, and in many cases, long forgotten sexual indiscretions, real or imagined. Lost somewhere in this maze of political correctness is the gut-issue role of our military. Their job is to break things and kill people. Besides, anyone who has ever been in the military can attest to the fact that keeping the western hemisphere free from aggression makes you horny.

I am particularly disgusted with Clinton's "Don't Ask, Don't Tell" policy. This shows just how shallow his understanding of the military really is. The only threat that I can see to having gays in the military lies in their susceptibility to potential espionage compromise, or blackmail, if you will. Since most gays are out of the closet these days, that potential vanishes. However, Clinton's policy just puts them back in the closet. He just took a non-problem and made it a big problem.

Dumb. "Hey Hillary, y'all watch this. Imo fix that queer thang overt DEE-fense".

I also feel pretty strongly about the right of women to serve in combat. I don't necessarily believe they should be in the trenches, but I see nothing wrong with them flying combat aircraft, serving on combatant ships, and serving in combat areas. To the Pat Schroeders of the world, who like to point to the number of women soldiers who were raped during the Gulf War, I say let's keep the *rapists* out of the combat area.

Early in the campaign, I wrote Gingrich a letter requesting "pre-appointment" to the National Security Committee, the old House Arms Service Committee if I was elected. My rationale was that this might help me in fund-raising efforts. I cited my twelve years of naval active duty and reserve service, as both an officer and an enlisted man, thirty three years as a government (Navy) contractor, and the fact that I held an engineering degree and understood weapons systems and government contracting. I've forgotten more than our Commander-in-Chief will ever know about the military. I pointed out that no one currently serving on that committee could match those credentials. He did this for Tillie Fowler (R-FL) when she was seeking re-election from Florida's Fourth Congressional District in Jacksonville, and it reportedly helped her.

Anyhow, I looked forward to addressing this veterans group because twelve posts were represented; everything from Homestead to Key West. I was also looking forward to bashing Clinton. I didn't do much of that in my campaign, because my opponent was Peter Deutsch, and I tried to stay focused. Probably the one thing that angered me the most about Clinton was when he tried to hide behind the Soldiers and Sailors Civil Relief Act of 1940 in his Supreme Court brief in his sexual harassment lawsuit with Paula Jones. This Act is designed to protect members of the armed forces from civil lawsuits while they are on active duty and potentially geographically unable to defend themselves at trial. Amid the wreckage of his thinking in trying to extract himself from the embarrassment of this particular episode, Clinton put forth the theory that since he was Commander-in-Chief, he was therefore on active duty and thus could not be brought up on civil charges until he got off active duty. Here is a self-admitted draft dodger, who has been quoted saying that he "loathed" the military, suddenly embracing the system to save his own political skin.

I felt this was a slap in the face of every man and woman who is now wearing, or who has ever worn the uniform. Apparently, five Medal of Honor winners felt the same way. These five wrote an open letter to the President, and it was published in the Washington Post, the Washington Times, the Atlanta Constitution, the LA Times, and a very few other papers on Memorial day of 1996. Because the letter did not receive wide coverage, many people never saw it. Well, I saw it, and I cut it out and saved it. I will share it with you below. I also read it to those veterans at that VFW meeting.

OPEN LETTER TO PRESIDENT CLINTON

Mr. President,

Please hear of those who wore with honor the uniform of our nation. Withdraw your use of the Soldiers and Sailors Civil Relief Act in your Supreme Court appeal.

It is distasteful irony that you would invoke the act at the time we remember those who gave their lives while wearing the uniform of the American military you once professed to 'loathe'.

To retreat from the call to arms and then later to embrace its code when it is convenient is an outrage to all who served and to those who remember the loss of those who paid the ultimate price.

It is neither our place nor desire to render judgment on the nature of the lawsuit before you, nor the legal basis for using the act in your defense. However, we cannot betray the memory of our fallen comrades by remaining silent on this issue. Your attempt to use a law designed for the brave men and women in uniform is indefensible.

s/
Pat Bride Maj. USA(Ret)

Earnest Children—Col. USA(Ret)
James Baker, Jr. MSgt—USA(Ret)
James Hendrix—MSgt—USA(Ret)
Elliot Williams—BMC—USN(Ret)

Most honorable men, given a public upbraiding such as this from five Medal of Honor winners, would quietly retire from public life. Clinton merely blew it off.

Keeping this engagement with the VFW caused me to miss a big Veteran's Rally back in Ft. Lauderdale. However, I was put in contact with the organizer of the rally, LtCol. Connie Connolly. I wish I had met Connie earlier because she is a conduit into every veteran's organization in South Florida. She is a nurse, and she is still very active in the Army Reserves. She graciously invited Sandy and me down to meet her Reserve Unit during one of her drill weekends, and we attended another meeting with a Vietnam veterans group at her invitation. Connie is one of the most exuberant people I have ever met, and her enthusiasm is absolutely contagious. However, the creek was really backing up on me, and I just didn't have time to develop all the contacts with who she would have put me. If I decide to do this again, Connie will be one of the first people I will try to get on my team.

One of our biggest TV debates was scheduled late in the campaign and the Greater Ft. Lauderdale Chamber of Commerce sponsored it. This debate included five congressional races with panelists from the Sun-Sentinel, the Miami Herald, and NationsBank, one of the sponsors. It was taped at the ComCast TV studios in downtown Fort Lauderdale, and was called "Cast Your Vote '96". In addition to the regular panelists, there was a contingent of high school students who would also be permitted to ask questions of the candidates. This was a taped show, to be aired on *all* cable stations in the area, easily the widest coverage we had had to date.

This was the *only* TV debate that I actually prepared for, and I was loaded for bear. I was going to do my damnedest to nail Peter on a number of issues. At every other appearance, I had listened to him tell outright lies about his voting record, things he claimed credit for, and things he was going to do in the next Congress, which I *knew* were all bullshit. When we had met before, more often that not I spoke first, and I rarely had a chance to rebut him. *Tonight was going to be the night.* I think we were going to get six questions, alternating going first, and then we would each have a three-minute wrap-up.

I'm here to tell you, we got the worst questions imaginable. There were two on environmental issues, and Deutsch is the certified tree-hugging darling of the environmental eco-terrorist group, two on education, which is not my most photogenic subject because I am dead set on abolishing the Department of Education, one on the tobacco industry, for crissake, and one on drugs. The question on drugs was served up by Buddy Nivens, a political reporter for the Sun-Sentinel. This question was the only one I could get my teeth into because I had built drug interdiction boats for the U.S. Customs Service, and I knew a lot about drug interdiction, or the lack thereof, under Clinton's unenlightened policies. I think Buddy knew this. The question on the tobacco industry was not my strong suite either, mainly because at the time, I was a smoker. Nevertheless, I did manage to say that I thought cigarettes should be classified as a narcotic and controlled. Sandy cringed when this question was asked. She envisioned a pack of cigarettes falling out of my pocket while I was answering it.

For the wrap-up, I went first. Since I had no chance to confront Deutsch during the questioning, I used my entire three minutes to attack Deutsch's voting record. I said that he kept telling everyone that he had voted for a balanced budget amendment, which was a lie, because he had voted against the resolution *four times*. I went on to say he kept telling everyone that he was for saving Medicare when he had voted against every plan to save Medicare that had reached a vote in the 104th Congress. I closed with the fact that he kept saying that his main interest was the Seniors, but that he had voted for a 35% increase in the tax on Social Security income and that when the Republicans put forth a plan to repeal that unfair tax, he had also voted against *that.*

Peter was more than a little tight-jawed when it came his turn to speak, and he spent his entire three minutes trying to defend the charges I had just made. As soon as the cameras were off us, he jerked off his lapel mike and stormed out of the studio, leaving his aide, good ol' Henry Hyphen, behind.

As I was leaving, I passed Karen Unger, Rep. Clay Shaw's perky Legislative Aide, and she said, "Boy, you really pissed him off."

"Yeah," I said, "And now that I've shut down the tobacco industry, I think I'll go out and have a smoke."

Probably the biggest mistake that I made publicly occurred at a candidate forum at the Pine Island Ridge Retirement complex in Davie, Florida, about a driver and five iron from where I live. The audience was about three-fourths Democrat, not a hostile audience, but not easy either. Nevertheless, I was doing quite well. It was another hand-held-mike-down-on-the-floor-among-the-folks type settings, and I was getting good questions from the fairly large audience. I was talking common sense and truth, and they appeared to be listening to what I was saying.

Then some guy in the audience asked, "What's your feeling on Newt Gingrich?"

Well now, I know better. Gingrich himself told me not to try to defend him or the Freshmen in my campaign. But, I did defend him, and an audience hasn't been lost any quicker since President Bush threw up on the Japanese Prime Minister at a State Dinner in Tokyo. I left there thinking maybe I just wasn't cut out for politics.

Canceling out that less than sterling performance, one of the high points in the campaign came the following weekend when Sandy and I were invited down to Marathon for a "Conch Reunion". "Conchs" are what long-time residents of the Keys call themselves, and one has to live there quite a while to be considered a "Conch". In fact, you are supposed to be a Conch just to go to the reunion. Nevertheless, Sandy and I were invited, and we went.

One reason we went was because I knew Mel Fisher would be there. Mel is "King Conch", and he had just sent me a $1000 check. I wanted to personally thank him, and I wanted to assure him that I intended to spend all of the contribution exclusively on advertising *in the Keys*. During the course of the festivities, which naturally included prodigious amounts of beer, Mel decided the next Congressman should be made a "Knight of the Conch Roundtable". This is not an honor to be taken lightly. There are very few knights on this roundtable, and I doubt if there are any who have never lived in the Florida Keys. I was so knighted and given a certificate. I was also deeply touched.

So much so, in fact, that a few days later when I was back down in the Keys buying TV and radio time, I made the following radio commercial for airing on WPIK, a country and western station that is a big favorite in the Keys:

> *Hi there, PIK'N fans. This is Jim Jacobs, a Knight of the Conch Roundtable, running for Congress against that Yankee lawyer, Peter Deutsch.*
>
> *The best line I ever heard is from an old Randy Travis tune called, "Is It Still Over?" In that song, Randy is trying to figure out why his girlfriend threw him out, and he says, "That lie I told you was just another way to say I love you by protecting you from the truth."*
>
> *Well, I'm tired of Peter lying to me to protect me from the truth. It didn't work for Randy and it won't work for Peter Deutsch. So if you think Peter is lying to you like I know Peter is lying to me, we ought to throw him out just like Randy's girl did.*
>
> *So, VOTE for Jim Jacobs in November. The Florida Keys needs Jim Jacobs for Congress*

I got a lot of positive feedback on this commercial.

This trip yielded a meaningful gesture by a good friend. It was going to be an extremely long day. I had to cut this commercial in Cudjoe Key at WPIK and buy radio spots, I had to buy TV time in Key West, and I had a very important endorsement interview with the Key West Citizen newspaper. Following all of that, we had another big debate in Big Pine Key that evening. We couldn't stay over because I had commitments back in Broward the following morning. To further complicate matters, Deutsch could not be at the debate until 9:30 PM because Clinton was in Miami that day, and I guess Peter was going to be one of his horse-holders.

Ed Clausner, my Treasurer and close friend, offered to drive us down. This might not sound like much, but I'm here to tell you that it is. The trip is almost 200 miles each way, and most of it is on the very congested U.S.1 Overseas Highway. Furthermore, endorsement interviews and debates really take it out of you. We didn't get home until after 1 AM, and Ed had to catch an early flight out the following morning for Houston. As brain-dead as I was, I'm not sure I could have made that last 100 miles if I had had to drive it myself.

I wasn't overly impressed with the fact that Deutsch had to be in Miami to be with President Clinton and couldn't' make it back down to the Keys until 9:30 PM. In order for us to be at the debate, we had given up an invitation to have dinner with Dan Quayle at the beautiful Intercoastal home of Larry and Sharon Day. Sharon is the Republican Executive Committeewoman for Broward County. Now, our party organization might have been in a state of relative disarray during this election cycle, but by God, we've got the best looking State Committeewoman in the entire State of Florida, and I haven't even met the other sixty-six. Nor is she merely another pretty face. She has been CEO of her own successful company, serves on many boards, is an excellent public speaker, and she is very active in a number of local charities. She and Larry are an extremely gracious couple. Frankly, I would rather miss dinner with Quayle than *have* dinner with Clinton.

I did feel that this was an important debate, because Peter and I had yet to meet in the Keys and Deutsch was under a lot of pressure there. Besides, the format included drawing sealed questions from a box, and we each also got to ask the other a "hard" question. This was our first meeting since the ComCast TV debate and I was curious as to what his attitude toward me would be. Actually, he was cordial, and the debate went well. I thought I got the best of it, but then, you always do. For my "hard" question, I asked him how we could believe that he could possibly be fiscally responsible when he was number 77 on the list of the 100 biggest spenders in Congress, a tidbit that I had picked up on the Internet. He struggled through it; something about there being a lot of obscure "lists" floating around Washington. In my rebuttal I mentioned that the list was prepared by the National Taxpayer's Union, hardly an obscure organization.

For his "hard" question, he asked me about my stand on the Assault Weapons Ban. Peter ought to fire his investigator. This wasn't a homerun, it was a groin-high line drive back through the pitcher's mound. There probably isn't a more concentrated group of pro-gun activists this side of the Pecos than the good people living in the Keys. Here is a group of citizens that consider themselves to be on the last remaining frontier. They feel they have been betrayed by the State of Florida and they are certain that the federal government has a master plan to seize their property and turn the entire Florida Keys into a National Park. The Conch Republic has seceded once from the Union and soon after the election formally declared war on the United States over the Florida Keys National Marine Sanctuary, *and Peter asks me a gun-control question.* I left there that night thinking that there really is a God.

This was also the first time I had been publicly asked my thoughts on the National Marine Sanctuary.

My answer was pretty much as already outlined elsewhere herein, and there was no mistaking the fact that I was strongly opposed to it, while Deutsch was very much in favor of it. Nevertheless, he reiterated the same statement he had made to the press a few days earlier. He vowed to support the will of the voters and support the outcome of the referendum. I sensed that the crowd supported my position, but they also took his promise aboard. This part of the Keys voted heavily against the Sanctuary on the Referendum on Election Day and his lie, both to the press and at this debate, probably cost me the majority vote in the Keys.

The final week of the campaign was a real ball-buster, as you might well expect, with six debates scheduled over a four-day period. On Monday, there was a schedule conflict with a candidate forum with the Jewish Women's Council in Plantation, Florida and the Institute for Retired Professionals at Nova University in Ft. Lauderdale. I didn't know which, if either, Deutsch would attend. I assumed it would be with the Jewish Women's Council, since he likes to beat that drum so much. I also figured there would be more potential votes at that meeting so I sent Ashley Keller, my seventeen-year-old political prodigy down to Nova. The IRP had said they would give us fifteen minutes, which is a rarity, and I knew Ashley had written a fifteen-minute speech especially for the occasion.

Deutsch showed up at the Jewish Women's Council, as I had predicted, and we went through our routine of him getting up and telling lies and me shooting holes in them. After we finished, Peter asked me if I was going down to Nova, and he asked me how to get there, since this forum was to be held on the East Campus in Ft. Lauderdale and he didn't know where it was. I gave him directions and he took off in a cloud of dust. I could have made it there, just as he did, but I was feeling bad about Ashley not getting to give his speech on which I knew he had spent a lot of time preparing. Besides, I was getting tired of Peter. Listening to all his lies is sort of like wrestling with a pig in the mud. After a while it occurs to you that the pig is enjoying it. I hung back and took my time getting there, and Ashley was speaking when I arrived. One of the officials came up and said they would give me five minutes when he finished, should I wish to add anything. I thanked him but told him that Ashley was speaking for me. He literally blew Deutsch away.

After the meeting, Ashley and I were standing outside when Peter came up and congratulated him and asked him how old he was. Ashley replied that he was seventeen. Peter then asked him why he wasn't in school and Ashley replied, "Because Mr. Jacobs asked me to cut class and be here."

The kid is not only sharp but he tells the truth. I fully expected to read in the papers that I was contributing to the delinquency of a minor. While the three of us were standing there, two gentlemen came up and told Peter they were not going to vote for him; that Ashley had convinced them that they should vote for me. The kid felt about ten feet tall. Peter, if I don't get you, Ashley will get you one of these days.

Something else interesting happened that day. As I was driving down to Nova, I noticed that my signs were still up along State Road 84, the route I had advised Deutsch to take. The signs had been up for about three weeks, a distinct rarity in this campaign. The average life of my campaign signs was about two days. I thought to myself that I should have sent Peter by another route, and mentally kicked myself in the butt. Sure enough, the next day all my signs along the route were gone.

I bought 1500 signs during the campaign, thinking that signage would be a good "bang for the buck" in getting my name out because I was so unknown. Furthermore, except for about 350 signs that I sent down to the Keys, and some that went to South Dade, I built all of my own signs. I remember remarking to a reporter that I was probably the only congressional candidate in the country building and installing his own signs. This got printed somewhere. I had offers of help, but actually building the signs was a sort of therapy. Whenever the pressure would mount, or if I just got pissed off about something, I would go out in the driveway and build thirty or forty signs. It worked like a charm.

Stealing campaign signs is about as unsavory as you can get. Given my limited financial resources and the fact that I built and installed most of them myself, it was particularly unsettling. One Saturday, Murphy Hanley, one of my "eagles" and I replaced about fifty signs that had disappeared. Every sign that we re-installed that day we put right in the middle of a hill of fire ants. For readers who are not familiar with this breed of ant, they are vicious and have been known to kill cattle. Frankly, I would rather get hit by a cottonmouth. Our theory was that if the fire ants didn't get the perpetrator when he was snatching the sign, there would be fire ants on the sign when it was thrown in the trunk of the car, infesting the vehicle. I would like to claim credit for the idea, but I cannot. This was all Murphy's idea. I went to sleep that night with a smile on my face.

The day Sandy and I drove down to Marathon for a Conch Reunion, my signs were up all the way down along U.S.1, courtesy of John Donnelley. We retraced the route on the following Tuesday when Ed Clausner drove us down and every single sign was down. Everyone else's signs were still up. Deutsch was in the Keys that day because we had a debate that evening. I am not saying that he personally stole the sign; even Peter is smarter than that. But I do think he was behind it. Well, I was told that he was ruthless and would stop at nothing.

We had the same problem around Homestead. Some NRA volunteers in South Dade were building and installing the signs, and they would use a ladder to place them very high up on telephone poles. The life of the signs was about two or three days, and again, my signs were the only ones missing. Of the 1500 signs purchased, I doubt if fifty were left standing on the day of the election.

On Tuesday of the final week, the Sun-Sentinel came out with an article with Deutsch making personal attacks against me. I had received a heads-up by Deborah Rameriz, the reporter doing the story, and she factually reported my answers to the charges. His charges were all smoke, but we had gotten through almost the entire campaign without personal attacks. He charged that I was operating a business out of my home without a proper business license, and my answer was that there isn't a business license for what I do. He next charged that I had been living full time in Washington while claiming a homestead exemption in Florida, which was more smoke and easily deflected. Lastly, he said that I had improperly filled out an FEC form, misstating my campaign contributions. This was the error I mentioned earlier when I filled out the forms myself. This had long been reconciled with the FEC to everyone's satisfaction. Nevertheless, Deutsch was screaming that I should be disqualified for this dastardly transgression.

What made this particular charge somewhat comical was the fact that he made it at exactly the same time that the shit was hitting the fan with the millions of dollars in illegal campaign contributions from the Indonesians and Buddhist monks that were greedily accepted by the Democratic Party. Deutsch was all but pounding his shoe on the podium demanding in the newspapers that I be disqualified for filing a false report. By the way, my cash-on-hand bottom line in that report was $367. At that time, Deutsch had almost a million dollars in his campaign account.

Also perplexing was the fact that we had been receiving a lot of contributions from the Keys drawn on corporate accounts. These were $100 and $200 contributions, mostly from fishermen and real estate people, who didn't know that corporate checks were not acceptable. It was also at a time when we were trying to scrape together every dime we could get our hands on for TV spots. Ed Clausner, my Treasurer, is probably the straightest guy that ever picked up a campaign checkbook, and there was just no way he would cash these checks. Instead, we had to go back to the people involved and try to get a personal check. In fact, I will go on record right here and say that my campaign account was the squeaky-cleanest campaign account in the nation in the 1996 election cycle, not because of me, but because of Ed.

Nevertheless, this change of tactics to personal attacks caused a flag to go up, and I didn't know what else he might come up with on the eve of the election. The only way I could protect myself was to get an ad on TV making him look like a cheap-shot artist for making personal attacks, and try to broad brush it enough to cover anything else he might come out with. To show how absolutely responsive Jones Intercable was, from the time I decided that I needed to make another commercial until I had the new commercial *in the can* was a little over three hours. I will assure you, there is not a political organization in this country that could match that.

We decided to go with a variation on the rattlesnake commercial, and used much of the same footage, just shooting me live for a short segment. I have reproduced the storyboard below:

VIDEO	VOICE OVER
Rattlesnake (Existing Footage)	This is a rattlesnake
Peter Deutsch (Existing)	This is Peter Deutsch. Peter has raised almost a million dollars, mostly from special interest groups. He has outspent Jim Jacobs by 15 to 1. And yet, he has chosen to attack Jim personally.
Rattlesnake striking (Existing Footage)	This snake is deadly. It can kill you.
Peter Deutsch (Existing)	Peter is a nuisance.
Jacobs (Live) Logo	I have attacked Peter Deutsch on the issues. He has chosen to attack me personally. A simple mis-take on a filing form. A business license that is not required. A perfectly legal second home. And who knows what else?
Jacobs (Back Live)	Come on, Peter. Let's get with the issues.
Jacobs walks off mumbling	God, what a pain in the a..

I really liked that rattlesnake. I had the ad on the air the next day, and it ran off and on in sequence with the other three ads for the few remaining days until the election. I don't know if he planned more of these cheap shots or not, but nothing else appeared in print.

Of the four debates remaining, two were with a friendly group and two were with a hostile group.

The "friendlies" were both being sponsored by the Florida Reform Party. Pauline Kline is the Reform Party Area Coordinator and we had met previously on several occasions. I always made it a point to attend their meetings when invited, and we had been invited on two previous occasions. I had been asked to speak both times. On one of these occasions my new friend, May Choate, the Reform Party non-candidate was present. This was not really a debate, but more of a roundtable discussion of all the things that needed changing in our government. The Reform Party would endorse a congressional candidate, and I wanted that endorsement badly. The first debate was in Broward, and Deutsch and I were invited to debate each other.

This was one of the better debates that we had because Pauline gave us plenty of time and allowed several rebuttals. The Reform Party is quite conservative, and I sounded a lot like Ross Perot in my beliefs and ideas. Peter started with the personal attacks again, but he had no way of knowing about the commercial I had made that day. I deflected it the same way I did in the commercial, and I don't think he won any points with the audience. Once again, he served up the assault weapons ban, and once again I hit it out of the park, this time getting spontaneous applause. On taking a "hard question", the goal is to just get through it. You're not supposed to hit a home run.

On my way out the door that evening, Pauline confided to me that I was going to get the endorsement. I don't know if the personal attack did it or not, but it didn't hurt.

The following evening, the Reform Party had another debate in Marathon, halfway down the Florida Keys. This one was for all the candidates, and Peter didn't even show up or bother to send a surrogate. He didn't want any part of me with this audience. I requested and received Peter's time, which gave me about twenty minutes. I used a good part of that time to come out strongly against the Marine Sanctuary, and received an uplifting response. I also got a question from the audience about Newt Gingrich, and this time I got it right.

I said, "Newt, who? Listen, I am running this campaign and he is running his. He's not helping me in this race, and I have no intention of trying to defend him or his record." Right answer.

On the Thursday before the election, Bob Dole finally made it to South Florida. Jack Kemp had been here a couple of weeks before, and not only were the congressional candidates not invited to share the stage with him but we were *specifically uninvited.* His advance team said we could show up and hand out literature. Well, the hell with him. I didn't need him to do that. To date I had probably faced less than 500 people in a live environment. This audience was at least that large. This snub generated about thirty more *very well built* signs.

Dole's visit was quite different. I was invited to attend and *maybe* sit on the stage, depending on who else was in attendance. There wasn't room on the stage, but we were treated very well, and Sandy and I were given prominent seats on the front row. We were "bumped" by Senator Mack and the two unopposed Republican candidates, Iliana Ros-Lehtinen, and Lincoln Diaz-Balart. I could certainly live with that. However, one of my signs made it onto national TV on the evening news. I think I had two signs in the entire audience of about 400 people, and one of my NRA supporters and one of my "eagles", Mike Padykula, managed to block the whole camera angle with the sign during one of the pans of the crowd. I don't know how this survived the editing process, but it did.

While waiting for Dole to make his appearance, Ileana Ros-Lehtinen and Lincoln Diaz-Balart both came over and introduced themselves and wished me luck. After Dole's speech, in which he announced his 96 hour marathon campaign finale, he was working his way around the roped off area greeting supporters who had rushed forward to shake his hand. Sandy and I were stuck about three people deep outside the ropes. Ileana spotted us and pulled us inside the ropes and introduced me to Senator Dole as a congressional candidate. Dole asked me whom I was running against and I told him. "Get rid of him," he said.

I felt that Congresswoman Ros-Lehtinen really went out of her way to make that introduction. She is another class act.

Not that there is any comparison whatsoever between a congressional campaign and a presidential campaign, but I could not help but notice the stark differences. I doubt if Dole spoke anywhere without all the orchestrated, cheering supporters, the bands, signs, and wild applause after even a banal comment. In fact, I'll bet he never even spoke to a Democrat, so tightly is everything controlled and orchestrated at that level. If he thinks he might encounter a hostile crowd, he just goes to a basketball game instead. On the other hand, we faced them all.

The final debate was, I would say, a hostile audience. It was held at the Century Village Retirement Community in Broward County, wherein reside 13,000 registered Democrats and 700 registered Republicans.

I used my allotted three minutes to tell all these seniors what fun and games "Mr. Wonderful" had been playing with their Social Security checks, and I put the amount of the tax increase in terms of dollars they could have used for airline tickets to go bounce the grandchildren on their knees.

I got one question from a woman, who took a good two minutes to totter up to the microphone. Her question? "How many Republicans voted for that tax increase you just talked about?"

Man, this was better than Peter's perennial question on the Assault Weapons Ban. "Not.......*ONE,*" I replied, letting it reverberate off the roomful of thick hollow skulls.

"How can that be? It is a Republican Congress. It could not have passed without at least some Republican votes," she opined.

"No, dear, this was in 1993, and it was a Democratic Congress, and not one Republican House Member voted for it, and not one Republican Senator voted for it, and *every* Democrat in both Chambers voted for it," said I.

"I don't believe you," said she.

"Well, ma'am, there sits your Congressman. If you don't believe me, let's ask him," I said, gesturing toward Deutsch. "Peter, what was the vote on that bill?" I asked.

Peter mumbled something about the fact that it was a vote along party lines. At least he told the truth. The old lady took another two minutes to get back to her seat, and I was out of there. I'd love to see Bob Dole handle that one any better. I still only got 6% of the vote in that precinct. I walked away from that place thinking that even Red Buttons couldn't get elected in a Century Village condo if he was a Republican.

I was feeling so good just to be out of there that I didn't even mind the next stop later in another, smaller, retirement community. This audience would boo Republican children at an Easter egg hunt. I was tired of talking to liberal voters and I was tired of talking to Peter. I was just tired, period.

The last shot that I fired just before the election was a good one. The Ft. Lauderdale Sun-Sentinel always delivers the morning paper in a transparent "sleeve" to keep the paper from getting wet. They also have a white, non-transparent sleeve that will take an ad or a message of some type. There was a six-week lead time to contract for this service. I had contracted to have a replica of my campaign sign logo printed on the sleeve, and I reserved the day before the election to have it appear. On the day before the election, 53,000 of these landed on doorsteps and in the driveways in West Broward. I don't know if Peter retrieves his own paper from his driveway each morning or whether he has an aide like Henry Hyphen come over and fetch it for him. Either way, his day was off to a less than rousing start.

I had given it my best shot.

8

ELECTION DAY

Basically, only one thing remained to be done on Election Day and that was to put up as many signs as possible at the polls. I had held back thirty or forty signs just for this purpose. Holding them back was the only way I could be sure of having any signs to put out at the polls, the way my signs had a penchant for disappearing. The night before, I had gathered up all the ones I could find in Broward County, which couldn't have been over fifteen signs. Out of the original fifteen hundred, that was not very many.

Dr. Murphy Hanley, the noted local podiatrist of fire ant fame, and a member of my Executive Committee, and I started about 5 AM. By noon we had placed signs at about fifty precincts. I don't know if this does any good or not, but I do know that a great majority of voters make up their minds about who to vote for in the two weeks before the election. I can only assume that there are a good percentage of voters who arrive at the polls still unsure. My rationale was that it wouldn't hurt to have my name out there as the last thing these voters saw as they entered the polling place.

In spite of what I consider a low voter turnout for a presidential election, we visited one precinct at about 7:30 AM and there was a line of about thirty people standing in the rain waiting to vote. I remember thinking that maybe there was hope for this country yet.

Actually, the turout appeared to be very heavy, but what did we know? Our database for this type of observation was "one". Of course, we were listening to Adam Clatsoff, "Captain Truth", on the car radio, and we called in. He took the call. I told him that it looked like a big voter turnout, and he asked me if they were Republicans or Democrats. I told him that they had to be Republicans because they looked like they were on their way to *work*.

I guess there *are* some Democrats out there not on welfare because they swamped us at the polls.

I think the tendency is, even on Election Day, that there is still something one could be doing. Well, if there was, I couldn't come up with it, so I went home and "crashed". I slept the afternoon through.

I knew that the only way that I could possibly win was to win big in the Keys and to have a small Democratic turnout and a large Republican turnout. I knew the Republican "Victory '96" group had been working around the clock almost, to "get out the vote". I had no idea what the Democratic counterpart had been doing, but I had to assume they were doing the same thing. At any rate, I felt that the Keys vote was the one I needed to win by at least 75% to offset the condo vote in Broward County. I was hoping for a "push" in Dade County, but I had done almost no campaigning there. I also knew that Harry Sawyer, the Monroe County Supervisor of Elections, would have a final count of the Keys vote within an hour of poll closing.

Accordingly, we delayed our departure for the Republican "Victory Party" until I received word on the Monroe County vote. As advertised, Mary Sawyer called me from Election Headquarters in Key West at eight o'clock on the button. There was good news and there was bad news. The bad news was that I only received 45% of the vote, far less than I needed to have any chance at all of offsetting the condo vote in Broward County. The good news was that the Marine Sanctuary had been defeated convincingly by 55% to 45%.

This swing occurred in the two weeks before the election. Back when the polls were showing that the referendum would pass with 60% in support of the Sanctuary, all my key supporters in the Keys felt that I should try to stay to the middle on the issue. Regardless of the outcome of the referendum vote, the State of Florida had to ratify the plan, as did the Congress. We all agreed that there was little I could do about the ultimate outcome as a candidate. In order for me to impact the ratification, I had to win the election, pure and simple. To do that, I needed at least 75% of the Keys vote, and bucking the polls on the Sanctuary issue would not give me that vote. Hence, we waited as long as we could. In retrospect, we waited too long, and the swing voters did not have enough time to connect me with the opposition to the Sanctuary. Even the Guest Editorial that the Key West Citizen allowed me to write, and which they printed on the Sunday before the election, wasn't able to overcome the timing problem. This article is reproduced in its entirety in the Appendix. Nor did we accurately predict the size of the swing vote, thinking it would be much closer. However, the biggest factor was Deutsch's promise to support the outcome of the referendum, and a lot of voters believed him.

I didn't believe him for a minute. I knew this was a lie because he was in the pocket of, and funded by, The Nature Conservancy, he owed his seat on the Commerce Committee to the Nature Conservancy, and his Legislative Aide in Key West was the wife of the Executive Director of The Nature Conservancy in Monroe County. The Nature Conservancy, the most formidable real estate conglomerate in the United States, with assets of over one billion dollars, has a vital stake in the sanctification of the Florida Keys, and it has nothing whatsoever to do with protecting the reef, or other environmental issues. Keeping *that* campaign promise would have been tantamount to Deutsch saying bullshit to the witch doctor.

Nor did he keep this promise. Less than a week after the election Deutsch reneged on his campaign vow and has since played a major role in getting the State of Florida to ratify the Sanctuary plan *against the will of the Monroe County voters.* Well, I was warned that the man is ruthless and would do anything to win. So he was and so he did.

Just as the Mighty Casey had struck out at bat, so had I, and there was no joy in "Mudville" as we prepared to go to the Victory Party. Just as we were leaving, Dan Rather, "Gunga Dan", as Jim Allingham calls him in his more benevolent moments, made the announcement that Bill Clinton had been declared the winner in the Presidential race, *with one percent of the vote counted.* I had to scrape Ashley off the ceiling.

Let's talk about this for a minute. Certainly, these pronouncements are made based on exit polls across the country that are gathered all during the day and fed into the network computers. Furthermore, I will concede that the network computer models are extremely accurate. However, I also think that the networks do an extreme disservice to the voters and the candidates in the states where the polls have not closed. All this matters not in the Eastern Time Zone, but it can have a profound effect in the Central, Mountain, and Pacific Time Zones, and it undoubtedly did. The networks argue that they have an obligation to report news as soon as they know it. While I agree with that, my position is that they don't *know* anything until at least 50% of the vote is counted, and even then, there are many races in doubt until the very end. I would hope that in the next election, if the networks won't get together and stifle themselves, that they be enjoined to delay reporting any predictions or trends until *all* of the polls have closed.

The Victory Party, which is a dichotomy, was in full swing when we arrived, and we were greeted wildly by the crowd, the first posting having me at 44%. However, I knew that this was the Keys vote being reflected and that as soon as the condo vote kicked in the percentage wouldn't hold. It didn't hold. Nor did hardly any of the other Republican candidates fare any better. We only won two races in the entire county and neither of those candidates was present. It was a short party.

How did I feel? Of course I was feeling let down. But, I was let down for my supporters. I *knew* that this quest was the biggest long shot that I had ever undertaken, but there were those who were absolutely convinced that I would win. For those, and you know who you are, I am eternally grateful for your faith in me.

I guess the most salient indicator that it was all over occurred when we got home. There is an old saying that silence is the sound of one hand clapping. Well, I'll coin another one. Silence is the sound of your fax machine on the night of a losing election.

How do I feel now, a few months after the election? I think just being a candidate for the United States Congress is, by far, the most important thing I have ever done. It was certainly one of the most interesting things I have ever done and I had a lot of fun doing it. Even though I was looked upon by many as being a "token candidate", I don't think I ran the race as one. I ran for what I absolutely believed, and somewhere along the line I managed to convince over 86,000 people to vote for me. That is fulfilling.

9

REFLECTIONS

At the end of every ocean salvage job and every ocean construction project in which I have participated over the past twenty years, we always sat down and put to paper the "lessons learned". In my opinion, this is an important step of any major project, because it brings to mind, and chronicles, both the mistakes and the triumphs. I think the word for this is *experience*. I think the same scenario is appropriate here.

First of all, I think our Founding Fathers and the Framers of the Constitution had in mind a citizen legislature, at least in the House of Representatives. I also think the American People would like to see such a concept evolve. This is evidenced by the fact that in the 104th Congress, almost two-thirds of the Freshman Class had little or no political background. This was almost a one-time occurrence, fueled by the "angry, white, male, middle class, majority" that propelled so many first time Republicans into office. Even though half of the prospective candidates with whom I attended Candidate School had similar backgrounds, not nearly as many were successful in the 1996 Election. Accordingly, I cannot yet call this a "trend". I think the trend is there, it is just not sustainable in light of the tremendous advantage incumbency generates for the sitting Members.

Certainly, incumbency is a distinct advantage in all forms of competitive endeavors, be it government contracting and procurement, the world in which my career has been based, or even retail sales, such as automobiles and real estate, where "call trade" separates the very successful from those who barely make a living in the first few years. But, nowhere is the advantage of incumbency so skewed as in national politics. The reasons are many, ranging from the franking privilege to access to campaign funds. Even in between the two, it all equates to *money*. It would cost a non-incumbent approximately $80,000 to put a piece of mail into every home in the district in which I have just run using bulk mail rates. An incumbent congressman can to this a couple of times a year for free, including the envelope stuffing and mail handling. Of course, this literature cannot be campaign related, but whom are we kidding? A "personal" letter from your congressman telling you of all the wonderful things he is doing for you tends to go a long way when it is time for re-election. This is one reason why 90% of incumbents are re-elected.

Before we can even approach a citizen legislature, we must have two ingredients: Term Limits and Campaign Finance Reform. Both will be hard to achieve.

TERM LIMITS

Seventy nine percent of voters responding to a national poll said they would like to see some form of Term Limits. Term Limits was one of the ten reforms proposed under the Contract with America, and it was the only reform that failed to pass the House in the first 100 days. Furthermore, this was merely a resolution requiring only a majority vote. Had this resolution passed the House *and* the Senate, it would then have had to be drafted into a Constitutional Amendment, which requires a two-thirds vote for passage. This is just not going to happen without relentless prodding from the voters themselves. Of course, the voters already have the ultimate "term limiter"; the vote. But this is usually reserved for some Member who commits a fatal faux pas somewhere that gets him or her un-elected.

There are two workable plans floating around, either of which have merit. The first is for each state to require that an indication be placed on the ballot next to each candidate's name attesting to their willingness to submit to Term Limits. In the case of an incumbent, this indication would be lifted from his voting record on the issue. For a challenger, the indication would come from a binding pledge to vote for Term Limits if elected. To enact this would require action by each State Congress, but many states already have Term Limits at the state level. This plan is entirely feasible and would be a handy guide for those 79% of voters out there who profess to be serious about the issue.

Of course, there will always be a few like Peter Deutsch. Peter voted FOR Term Limits on the Contract with America, one of a very few Democrats to do so. However, I submit that he was pretty sure that the measure would not pass on a Resolution, and he knew damn well it would never receive the two-thirds majority to enact it into law. Furthermore, if it came to a Constitutional Amendment vote, he could change his vote with impunity. However, this ploy gave him bragging rights in our campaign, which effectively blunted my binding pledge of a self-imposed six year Term Limit. This is why I support the ballot indicator because this scheme has some teeth, in that it would put guys like Deutsch's nuts in a vise with the voter's hands on the turnscrew. As the old saying goes, "when you have them by the balls, their hearts and minds shall follow."

Representative Bill Archer (R-TX), the Majority Whip, is also advancing a plan that would tend to place limits on the time one *will be willing* to serve in Congress. He described his plan during one of the GOPAC Wednesday night conference calls. He comes at it from a different direction involving congressional pensions. Under Archer's plan, each Member would only be allowed to accrue pension "multipliers" for the first twelve years they were in Congress. At today's salary levels, this would limit a Member's maximum pension to $27,500 per year upon retirement, still not a bad pension for twelve years of service. The Member could stay in Congress for as long as he could get re-elected, but his pension would be limited to that maximum. The beauty of this plan is that it only requires a majority vote to become law, rather than an unattainable two-thirds majority. I suggested on the conference call that he include in the plan a provision to *take away* a year's multiplier for every year a Member stayed past twelve years, but he didn't buy it.

I'm sure that every Member who has ever been elected goes to Congress with the purest of intention. But, somewhere within the heady atmosphere of *power*, most mortal men tend to "go native". I am a mortal man, and I decided early on that I would not give myself the chance to go native and that is why I declared the self-imposed Term Limit on myself.

Those in the Congress who are openly against Term Limits cite the need for "experienced" national legislators, and the benefits derived for a state or district that has a member of their delegation chairing a powerful committee. Well, it was this cadre of "experienced legislators" that got this country in the sorry shape that it's in. This country is almost $5.0 *trillion* in debt.

One example that I used many times during the campaign in criticizing the national debt was to define "trillion". Actually, I borrowed this from Bill Archer.

If one opened a business the day Jesus Christ was born, and was so inept that he managed to lose a million dollars each day, seven days a week, he still would not have lost one trillion dollars. Yet, we are *$5.0 trillion* in debt. If this takes experienced legislators to achieve, I submit we need less of them.

I've actually got a theory as to what is really the root cause of this $5 trillion debt. It is *air conditioning*. Think about it. The summer months, from June through September, are brutally hot and humid in Washington. We haven't had deficit-free balanced budget in almost thirty years, and the entire $5 trillion dollar debt has been accumulated since that time. If the Capitol wasn't air conditioned, all the Members would go home during these four months and spend their time constructively finding out what all is pissing off their constituents. They not only would become more in touch with the voters, but there would be four months that they wouldn't be sitting around the Capitol thinking up schemes to spend taxpayer's money. This hiatus would cut spending programs by a third, just based on time alone. A one-third cut in sure-to-fail socialistic spending programs would not only balance the budget, it would create a surplus. Actually, Lamar Alexander had something like this in mind, advocating a part-time Congress. He just didn't pinpoint the root cause. Had he done so and articulated it, he would probably be in the White House today.

Another common practice employed by almost all members of Congress, and at which Peter Deutsch was particularly adept when discussing the budget, is what I call deficit manipulation. This is sort of the boolean algebra of politispeak when it becomes necessary to toss numbers around. It always amazed me when I would get up and try to explain to the voters how deeply in debt this country had become under over forty years of a Democratic Congress, often citing Bill Archer's excellent example of $5.0 trillion. Deutsch would then get up and talk about how much he and the Clintonistas have cut the deficit during the past four years, while I am sitting there *knowing for a fact* that a third of this national debt has occurred on Clinton's watch. Actually, "cutting the deficit" and "trimming the national debt" are two completely different things. Democrats never, ever discuss the latter because it has never, ever happened in the past forty years. On the other hand, cutting the deficit is a feel-good topic that liberals throw out with wild abandon. It works like this.

Suppose Congress passes a budget appropriation of $1.8 trillion to run the government for the year. The Government Printing Office distributes this in that phone book sized publication called the 199? Federal Budget that all government contractors run down and buy to see what programs are funded so they know what programs to bid on. In a few months, the Office of Management and Budget (OMB) issues a report that says, "Uh-oh, we predict a revenue shortfall of $300 billion due to the famine in Outer Mongolia", or something similar. They never announce a budget overrun caused by Congress not being able to resist the urge to spend *your* money. The culprit is always the taxpayer who doesn't pay enough taxes. With this unwelcome, dire announcement, Congress scurries around "cutting waste". Now, let's pause right here for a minute.

Why would any rational individual "cut waste"? You *eliminate* waste. Anyhow, Congress cuts waste by taking $100 billion out of some vital defense program, usually one that is under budget and ahead of schedule and, Viola! Each Democratic Congressman and Senator can go home and tell the voters how they and Bill Clinton cut the deficit by $100 billion. Of course, no one ever mentions that the $200 billion budget overrun just gets added to the $5+ trillion debt for our children and grandchildren to pay. It's sort of like a family running up $5000 in *unpaid* credit card debt in each of four consecutive years. In the fifth year, the family "cuts waste" and only adds $3000 to the mounting debt that now reaches $23,000 in unpaid credit card debt. "Hey, honey, we cut our deficit by 40% this year. Let's go out and buy you a new fur coat."

Anyhow, I couldn't even seem to explain a vicious attack on Social Security income to senior citizens. How in the hell can I explain national debt to voters with their head in the sand?

CAMPAIGN FINANCE REFORM

I was probably the most under funded *serious* congressional candidate in the entire country. I spent $30,000, every cent I had. Of this I put up about $4,000 and the NRCC put up $10,000, so I "raised" only about $16,000. With this, I received over 86,000 votes, enough for election in some districts. This, by the way, comes to about $.35 per vote, easily a national record. By way of contrast, it has since been reported that the sugar industry spent $7 per vote in defeating the sugar tax issue. What this means is that I am either one lousy fundraiser, or one hell of a candidate. I think neither.

The truth is, I'm probably a pretty good fund-raiser; I was just unable to raise any funds. This is no more of a paradox than is the reason I was unable to raise any significant funds. If one would examine every congressional race, one would find than in 95%, the candidate that spent the most money won the election. Furthermore, in about the same percentage of races, the closer the two candidates were in money spent, the closer were the races. There are several reasons for this, all of which are quite logical.

Most basically, most major contributors know this, and most major contributors want to back the winner. PACs are the most major of all contributors. The first thing a PAC looks at is incumbency, the next thing is how well funded is the challenger. Nor am I criticizing this. PACs are a business and they are run like a business. Businesses that back losing products do not stay in business. PAC dispensers who back losing candidates do not keep their jobs. However, if a challenger is very well funded, he will receive PAC money, if for no other reason than it spells "insurance", in case the challenger does get in.

I don't know how many PACs who turned me down also told me that they hoped I beat Peter Deutsch. And I think they meant it. The problem was, they didn't think I *could* win. And they were absolutely correct.

There are exceptions, of course. The Christian Coalition and the NRA would never give money to Peter Deutsch. But, even with my 85% rating with the Christians, against Deutsch's 15%, or with my 'A' rating with the NRA against Deutsch's 'F', neither gave me a dime, because they knew I could not win.

It is the same with the media. The media equates money in the bank with the seriousness of the candidate. I was not considered a serious candidate by those in the media because of the size of my campaign fund. In fact, most of the earned media that I received centered around the disparity in money. Not once did the media say that I was not qualified or that I would not make a good congressman. In fact, they printed quite the contrary, as has been shown, but they didn't think the race would be close; therefore, the race did not rate much earned media.

I did not complain about this during the campaign, and I am not complaining about it now. What I am saying is that if there is ever to be a true citizen legislature, and if there is ever to be a stream of good, intelligent, qualified candidates making it into Congress, there first needs to be campaign finance reform and some form of Term Limits.

Put me in a race with Peter Deutsch with equal money to spend and I will spot him 10% in voter registration, and I will win.

Furthermore, I think Deutsch epitomizes precisely what is wrong with the system. He had approximately $400,000 in his campaign account when the race started and he raised another $600,000 plus during the race. Over 60% of this is Special Interest money. He is in the top 10% of fund-raisers in the Congress, and he is only in his second term. Furthermore, he chairs no committees, has sponsored no major legislation, and if such a rating existed, I would expect to find him with a lack-luster, if not a substandard rating as a congressman. There is no way that a Member with his lack of political stature can raise that kind of money without working at it almost full time. How much time does he spend, then, actually representing his constituents? There are only so many hours in a day.

I mentioned this to a reporter one day and was accurately quoted in the ensuing article. Deutsch's response was that I just didn't understand what being a congressman was all about. Well, Peter, I think being a congressman is about tending your flock.

Another thing that I think is interesting with Peter is that, even with the disparity in campaign funds between us, he never let up on the fundraising. I read some of his fundraising letters that went to the small contributors, the retirees living in the condos and other grassroots contributors, and they would have been comical had they not been so blatant.

Quoted below are excerpts from one of these letters:

"Now is not the time to become complacent and let the Extremist Right-Wing of the Republican Party run circles around us. Their spending is at an all-time high and the Special Interest PACs are trying to drown out the voices of the American people."

"My opponent has been carefully hand picked and is being funded by Newt Gingrich and the Extremist Right-Wing" (I wish, ED)

"Breaking the grip that Newt Gingrich and special interests have on Congress and freeing America from deadlock isn't going to be easy—that's why I need your help!"

"Your financial support is urgently needed if we are to help defeat those Extremists and continue to fight for the American family."

"Less than 75 days remain in my campaign. Please send as generous a contribution as you can to the **Peter Deutsch for Congress Campaign** *today. In this race, your dollars will go a long way toward helping me win this critical election."*

At this point in time, he must have had over $700,000 and he was still after the $10 and $20 contributions.

Even the Sun-Sentinel chided Deutsch in a post election article on fundraising written by Jill Miller, of their Washington Bureau. She questioned his need to raise so much money against such an under funded candidate. His reply:

" My opponent was somewhat of an enigma. For all he knew, Deutsch said, Jacobs could have had a personal stash of campaign cash. Until the very end, I didn't know if I was dealing with someone who was going to spend $100,000 or a million dollars."

So, what is the answer on campaign finance reform? Numerous suggestions have been proposed. Getting Congress to pass serious campaign reform is like getting them to enact Term Limits. Why should a sitting Member vote to drastically reduce this significant advantage? I think it has to be done for them, by pressure from the voters and from the Federal Election Commission.

Nor are PACs and lobbyists necessarily bad. Lobbyists play a very vital role in our legislative process. A congressman cannot stay "up" on every single issue, and many times needs nuances of certain issues explained to him and his staff. Doing away with PACs and Lobbyists is not the answer. However, the playing field should be leveled if there is ever to be any semblance of a citizen legislature who go to Washington for a limited period to do a job of representation for the constituents of their district that they have been sent there to do through the voting process, and then come home.

I even think "soft money", which is money that can be contributed to a political party, and not earmarked for a particular candidate, still should have a place in the funding of political races.

The nuts and bolts of how this all might work is probably grist for a book in itself. However, I do think the bottom line should be that the party nominees in the General Election for national office should be "given" a certain amount of money with which to conduct their campaign and "given" a block of network airtime with which to run 30 second or one-minute spots. This would reduce the campaign to one of issues, candidate presence and presentation, and campaign management i.e., the biggest bang for the buck.

CAMPAIGN MANAGEMENT

There were a couple of points that served me well, and I got them from Joe Gaylord's book, "Flying Upside Down". Mr. Gaylord is a noted Washington, D.C. political consultant, and the book was published by GOPAC and was distributed at candidate school. In the book, he stresses the five 'C's for a challenger campaign; Confidence, Creativity, Contrast, Controversy, and Capital.

Certainly, I had plenty of *confidence*. As I mentioned early in this book, confidence has never been one of my short suits. I feel I was quite *creative*, because one cannot get through an entire congressional campaign on $30,000 without an ample dose of creativity. How many candidates write their own TV and radio advertisements, design their own signs, and, for that matter, write their own speeches? There was certainly *contrast* between Peter Deutsch and me. We didn't agree on much of anything. Probably the only *controversy* centered around the fact that I had no political background, and I tried to use that as an asset, stressing a business approach to government. The only 'C' that I seemed to lack was *capital*, and that is what did me in.

Another point that I took to heart was "staying on message". My platform was a Balanced Budget Amendment, fixing Medicare and Social Security, and less government and less taxes. Of course, I felt fully up on all issues, but I pretty much stayed on message except during questioning sessions, and even then I tried to build my answers around those cornerstones. Furthermore, the press never tripped me up and I never had to flip-flop on an issue because I was most comfortable with my stand on all the issues.

The third thing I took away from reading Gaylord's book was that an incumbent had to carefully manage his campaign, while a challenger could, and should, do anything he could get away with.

Actually, I think Deutsch did a good job of managing his campaign. He did this primarily by staying away from me. He would not debate unless he absolutely had to, and the fact that I didn't even meet him until one month before the election attests to his skill at avoiding me. I'm not sure that I would ever have met him had he not gotten some heat from the print media for avoiding me in a manner that was becoming obvious.

Nor, did I go off-the-wall. I made up my mind early that I was not going to run a negative campaign. By "negative", I mean that I was not going to attack him personally unless I was forced to. I feel that I attacked him vigorously on the issues and on his voting record, but I never resorted to personal attacks, as he did late in the campaign. In fact, Gaylord also said somewhere in his book to make sure your stick of dynamite was not shaped like a boomerang before you threw it.

The best example of this that I have ever seen took place in Hawaii years ago. It could have either been in the early sixties or the late sixties, I don't remember because I was living there both times. A Caucasian, Frank Fasi was running against a local, a man named Anderson for Mayor of Honolulu. This is almost as powerful an office as Governor in the Islands. Anderson had been slinging mud left and right throughout the entire campaign, and Fasi had run an absolutely clean race. The polls had the race at dead even.

At that time in Hawaii, before satellites, all TV was either local or canned. The evening news on the U.S. West Coast was taped and put aboard a United Airlines jet and flown to Honolulu every evening. This tape was then rushed to the TV studio and became the Late News every evening just before the station signed off the air. Right after the news, the station would play the National Anthem and show a clip of the American Flag with military jets passing overhead in formation, and then the screen would go blank. This routine never, ever varied.

The TV station had offered both candidates 15 minutes of free air time on election eve following the late news and before the familiar sign-off. Fasi was first. Fasi used the first ten minutes of his allotted time by just lowering the boom on Anderson, iterating every dirty trick that Anderson had pulled throughout the campaign. He then used the National Anthem/flyover sign-off clip that he had apparently taped and then let the screen go blank for the final three or four minutes of his allotted time. It is estimated that ninety percent of the viewers got up from their sofas, switched off the TV and went to bed, as had been their nightly ritual.

Of course, Anderson went berserk, but Fasi won the election by a little over one percentage point. Paybacks are hell!

THE BIG LIE

Probably the question I have been asked the most since the election was what actually surprised me the most about the political arena. From the first time I declared myself a potential candidate, and long before I actually decided to run, I had received six or eight fax sheets per day from NRCC on various issues. The format was usually pretty much the same with an issue; the Republican position, perhaps some "spin", and then the Democrat position. The latter was usually capped with More Of The Big Lie. I read the Washington Post and the Washington Times every morning and I knew the intricacies of most issues pretty well, and the Democratic position *did* usually seem distorted from reality. This is called *demagoguery* in politically correct Washington. This became even more pronounced in the 104th Congress where the Republicans were in control of the Congress for the first time in over forty years.

The Republican-led House was also cranking out legislation and various plans at an unprecedented rate, and the Democrats, with no plans of their own, could only sit back and take potshots, *always*, it seems, distorting the truth. I guess I took all this aboard, but I pretty much dismissed it as "politics as usual". "The Big Lie" reached a zenith on the subject of Medicare.

The Republican plan to avert bankruptcy of Medicare was basically a way to slow the *rate of growth* of Medicare spending from an empirically *projected* 10% per year to a projected 7% per year. The rationale for this, and it was sound, was that a 7% projected growth would be adequate for taking into account both normal inflation and *medical inflation*. Actual spending per recipient would increase from approximately $4800 per year in 1995 to approximately $7100 per year in the year 2002. There were also some other cost saving methods, such as offering other health care options such as HMOs, vouchers, et.al. The result would be a *savings* of $270 million per year that would render the program sound. There was also a "lock box" provision attached to all of this that dictated that *any* savings generated by this plan would stay "locked" in the Medicare Trust Fund. In other words, these savings could be used for nothing else other than Medicare.

Unfortunately, the Republicans were also trying to pass a tax cut, *which had nothing whatsoever to do with the plan to save Medicare.* Of course, the Democrats had no plan of their own to save Medicare. Furthermore, in the first two years of Clinton's Administration, with still a Democratic Congress, they did absolutely *nothing* about the looming crisis in Medicare, even though the Medicare Board of Trustees, who was appointed by Clinton, two of whom were serving on his Cabinet, and who were all Democrats, had warned of the impending crisis. It also goes without saying that the Democrats were opposed to any tax cut. Tax *cuts* are just not in the Democratic playbook.

The Democrats jumped on both plans and had a field day. "The Republicans are slashing Medicare in order to give a big tax cut to the wealthy," screamed the headlines, usually quoting that idiot, Dick Gephardt. They literally never let up. I cite this example for a reason.

Ole Nathan Naive here made this whole issue a focus of my campaign. I embraced this issue, because I knew the *truth*. All I had to do was get up and tell the voters the truth, exposing The Big Lie, right? Wrong!

First of all, as I said earlier, I probably only reached about 700 people directly at candidate forums during the campaign. Furthermore, as I have also pointed out, we were usually only given one minute to answer a question, or three minutes to define our platform. However, just as big an impediment to getting the truth out was Peter Deutsch, because he was campaigning just as hard to perpetuate The Big Lie.

I would charge that he voted against the plan to save Medicare. He would come back and say that the reason was because Newt Gingrich was slashing $270 million to give a tax cut to the rich and so on, and so on.

I heard him say time after time that he had voted for a balanced budget. He did vote for Clinton's flimsy, unworkable scam for a balanced budget plan, with *no teeth* in the Democratic controlled 103rd Congress. But in the 104th Congress, controlled by the Republicans, he voted against a meaningful plan to balance the budget *four times*.

He would get up and say that his biggest concern was the elderly and the senior citizens. But yet he voted for the biggest tax increase in the history of this country, which included the onerous provision of increasing the amount of Social Security income subject to federal income tax from 50% to 85%, a "hit" of approximately $700 per year on each of the people that could afford it the least. When the 104th Congress sought to repeal this tax in 1995, he voted against this repeal as well, casting a double whammy at the condo voters, among others, who sent him to Congress in the first place, and then sent him back again.

Deutsch would stand before an audience and say that during Clinton's first term, the federal deficit had been reduced each year. Another Big Lie. The federal deficit *increased* one trillion dollars during Clinton's first term. Remember how much a trillion dollars is? Now, the *rate* of deficit growth slowed during this time, but the rate of growth was in a runaway mode when he took over because of the free-spending Democratic Congress, the failed social programs of the Great Society, and the list goes on and on. In fact, the rate of deficit slowed the most during the last two years of Clinton's first term because we had a Republican Congress for the first time in over forty years.

What do you think the government shutdown was all about? It was about the Republican Congress wanting to reduce the rate of deficit growth to *zero* by cutting spending. Clinton vetoed it, shutting down the government. The Republicans did not shut down the government. Bill Clinton shut down the government. Try to tell that to the voters, because the Democrats do one thing better than anyone else. They lie more convincingly.

Peter loved to get up and portray himself as a fiscal conservative. One night, during the "hard question" phase of a debate, I asked him how he could portray himself as such when he was listed as number 77 in the National Taxpayer Union's list of the 100 Biggest Spenders in Congress. He stumbled through the answer with something about various obscure lists floating around Washington listing insignificant trivia. Well, the National Taxpayer's Union is hardly obscure, and the $61.6 billion in *new* spending that he supported is not trivia. Sending Deutsch back to Congress to be a fiscal conservative, as he portrays himself for the final two months of each election cycle, is like sending Dracula out to drive the Bloodmobile.

Whose fault is it that an entire political party can be built upon an underpinning of lies *and* still *prosper*?

I lay it all at the feet of the citizens of this country, *some* of whom are voters, a *few* of whom are *informed* voters, and *all* of whom are taxpayers. The taxpayers of this country are on a perpetual honeymoon because they are continually being fucked. At least on *my* honeymoon, I learned something new every day.

Perhaps the reason the Big Lie is able to grow and prosper is that the citizens expect all politicians to lie. This is far from an undeserved rap for career politicians, because most of them do lie, and they do it with impunity. I have dealt harshly with the Democrats in this book, but Republicans have their crosses to bear, as well. Richard Nixon comes to mind, as does more recently, Enid Waldholtz (R-Ut) and Wes Cooley (R-Or), neither of whom should have ever been elected in the first place, because they lied *to get in*.

At one forum, I was waxing eloquent about how the Democrats had stolen the entire Social Security Trust Fund, and replaced it with Treasury Bills. IOUs, if you will. One lady in the audience asked me if any Republicans might have had a hand in that. I had been coming at the issue from the standpoint that this happened on the Democrat's watch, during a Democratic controlled Congress. Of course, some Republicans had a hand in this. I squirmed out of it by saying that, "There were Democrats involved, and there were Republicans involved, but *I* wasn't involved". Not really good enough.

There has been much rhetoric in the Congress about congressional reform. To be sure, the 104th Congress passed a number of congressional reforms concerning the manner in which Congress does business on the very first day they were in session. There remains a lot more to do. Term Limits and Campaign Finance Reform are important first steps, but to truly reform our political systems will require massive proaction by the voters.

The only effective way to stop candidates from lying is to catch them in these lies. My feeble attempts to do this in the short time I had available in front of a very few voters was woefully inadequate. Those few who heard me probably assumed I was lying, too. The information that I was trying to disseminate wasn't obscure data that had to be dug out of some archive somewhere; it was public data. It was the *truth*. It was also untarnished by media bias.

Liberal bias in the media is a whole story in itself that I have no intention of getting into here, but I will say that I don't put all of the blame on the media. Most of the individuals that shape our news are liberals. Accordingly, they see things through liberal lenses and the output has a liberal spin. Nor is liberalism basically wrong any more that conservatism is basically right. But somewhere in the middle lies the truth, and in order for the voters to seek out the truth, they are going to have to get off their collective butts and *inform themselves.*

The best example of the Big Lie at the presidential level in the recent election concerned, again, Medicare. Untold millions voted for Bill Clinton over Bob Dole *because they were worried about the future of their Medicare.* My God! Although he did a terrible job of articulating it, *Dole* was the candidate who wants to preserve Medicare. Clinton had already tried to scrap the whole system with Hillary's folly of a national health care program that was so expensive that even the Democrats wouldn't support the plan. Of course the media widely reported that Bob Dole had voted against Medicare when it was formed in 1968, neglecting to report, however, that the reason he voted against it was that he supported an opposing system at that time which, in retrospect, was a far superior system than the Medicare plan we now have. Similarly, Gingrich was just as widely reported to have said that "We should let it just twist in the wind". He said that, all right, but he wasn't even talking about Medicare when he said it.

I think the single most important factor in the return of power to the Republican Party in 1994 was Rush Limbaugh. There was also a definite conservative spin on everything that came out of his mouth, but it was basically the *truth.* Even more important, what he had to say, and the way he said it, at least got the voters *thinking.* When one starts to think, the tendency is for that person to find out more about the question. This is called becoming *informed*. That is what has to happen if the voting public is to force congressional reform on the politicians.

The worst piece of legislation to come out of Congress since busing is the "motor-voter" law. This ill-conceived piece of trash law does nothing but swell the voter roles with uninformed voters, who will never be informed and whose only contribution to the process is to cancel the votes of those who are. People in other lands die by the thousands fighting for the *right* to register to vote, and then they stand in line for days to validate that right. I think there should be *some* effort required by a potential voter to gain the right to cast a ballot, and I don't think requesting an application, filling it in, putting a stamp on it and mailing it in presents any undue hardship. I also think that any-one who goes through even this simple wicket is a lot more likely to go to the polls than someone who has a card forced upon them and prob-ably doesn't even realize what they have just been handed. It is the same principle as grassroots campaigning. If someone signs your filing petition, or contributes $5 to your campaign, they have made an investment in you. Having made this investment, they will probably go the polls and vote for you.

In addition to becoming informed, I also think the voters must hold those they elect to office *accountable*. Oh, we hold the Waldholtz, the Cooleys and the Reynolds accountable for major gaffs, but the reason we send a representative from a congressional district to Washington is to represent *the interests* of the people of that district. I know I am beat-ing the 1993 Social Security Tax increase to death, but I am still mysti-fied by why the voters keep sending representatives back to Congress to keep picking their pockets. Allow me to try one more time, and to come at this from one more angle.

We have established that the Democratic Congress of the past forty plus years have "stolen" the Social Security Trust Fund and replaced it with Treasury IOUs. Having nothing left to steal, except the monthly payments coming in from all the businesses in the form of FICA "con-tributions", which are inviolate because they are needed to cover the following months Social Security checks, as in "paycheck-to-paycheck living", Clinton and his other dupes such as Deutsch, effectively found a way to steal a portion of what little was left of the Social Security Fund. This is done by *money laundering* in its purest form. This travesty was passed into law by the 1993 Democratic Congress, with every single Democrat in the House and Senate voting "for" the money laundering scheme, and every single Republican in the House and Senate voting "against" it.

It works like this: Since the Social Security Trust Fund is devoid of all cash, holding only Treasury notes that are redeemable by the American taxpayer (our children and grandchildren), there is nothing left to steal. Clinton and his followers found a way to steal a good portion of the monthly FICA revenues destined to pay the following month's Social Security checks by laundering a portion of the money from the Social Security Trust Fund, *through the Social Security recipients*, and back into the *General Fund*, in the form of additional income taxes on the monthly checks.

People go to jail for money laundering. Yet our Democratic Congress put the insideous plan in place in 1993, and I am sorry to say that our Republican-led Congress has so far failed to identify one of the slickest scams ever perpitrated on the American taxpayer, and especially on those who can least afford to lose a significant amount of a meager fixed income in involuntarily supporting more failing social programs.

The "fix" is woefully obvious. If our elected congressional leaders lack the nut-sack to repeal this insidious tax in its entirety, at least put a "lock-box" on the additional tax revenue and revert it back to the Social Security Trust Fund, rather that into the General Fund. This way you will only fleece our senior citizens, rather than fucking them. Aren't honeymoons wonderful?

There is no question that the most formidable voting bloc in the 20th District are the "condo voters", who typically vote 90% Democratic. Essentially, these voters actually dictate who goes to Congress from this district. Yet all it took was a phone call from President Clinton to Peter Deutsch in May 1993 and Deutsch sold out this entire voting bloc by voting to increase their federal income taxes by 35%, and paving the way for the biggest money laundering project in the history of our country.

As reported by the Miami Herald on May 28, 1993 on that phone call:

> *"At that point, we agreed that I didn't need to take up any more of his time," Deutsch said a few hours later. "He had a lot of other calls to make. I said, "Make sure you get your votes." The article goes on to say, "But for now, Deutsch is a loyal Democrat who hopes the folks back home will understand."*

Well, I'm a Senior, and I *don't* understand why a simple phone call, even from the President of the United States, would cause a congressman to vote against the best interests of the people that sent him up there to represent them. There must be accountability if there is to be reform.

POLLS

Polls should be outlawed. The Presidential Election was won in the polls because I think a vast number of voters are swayed by the polls. These are the uninformed voters, who don't know the first thing about the issues, but who are almost fanatic in their desire to be part of the winning vote. How else could the worst president we have ever had, and a man of the most questionable character that we have seen in major office in our lifetime, become re-elected? Here is a man who was a draft dodger, a pot smoker, a womanizer, an alleged sexual harasser, and who has been on the fringes of several special prosecutor criminal investigations almost from the day he took office. Here is a man who not only reneged on all of his campaign promises, but who did a 180 on most of them, and then, with no re-election plan of his own, stole the Republican agenda and ran on it, *and won*!

I would even like to be able to say that this was just the un-informed electorate that made this travesty happen, but even the un-informed voters aren't *that* stupid. No, I think it was the combination of the uninformed voters *and* the polls.

Furthermore, even the political pros rely much too heavily on the polls. Approach a PAC for money and the first question is, "Where are you in the polls?" Hell, if I had money for polls I wouldn't be asking them for money. Nor are polls inexpensive. Even the kind of poll that I would have needed would have cost $6000 to $8000, money that I think I spent much better elsewhere.

Deutsch ran at least one poll in our district, but he never released the results. This had to be because the poll showed the race closer than it was, or that he was so far ahead in the polls that releasing the results would have curtailed his needless fund-raising. I suspect it was the latter.

I'm not going to spend a lot of time on this subject because I am beating a dead horse. The *vote* should be the only poll, and I would like to return to the suspense of election night waiting for the last vote to be counted.

ELECTRONIC CAMPAIGNING

Will Connolly, a long-time friend and the Editor of the Broward Republican Executive newsletter has tested a theory that I find quite interesting. Will is also a committeeman of one of the precincts in my district. In two of the last five elections, not counting this one, Will sat down at the computer and wrote a personal letter to every Republican in his precinct, urging them to vote for his candidates, and giving a reason why they should do this. He then placed the letter in a plain envelope with his home return address on it, and put a *32 cent stamp* on it and mailed it. His theory is that most people throw away campaign literature mailed to them without even reading it. I certainly did this before I became involved in the process. He feels that a personal letter from a neighbor will be opened, and once opened and the first few lines read, even though it becomes apparent that it is political in nature, it will continue to be read by most people just because it is from a neighbor. The percentages between the election years when he did this and those elections when he did not are rather startling. His Republican voter response was up over 10% in those elections where he tested this theory. He did it again this election cycle, and we did quite well in his precinct. He did this only once in this election, and he included the entire slate of candidates in the letter.

Of course, this is time consuming because each letter must be individually printed on an envelope, but with computer mail-merge, it is manageable. I did something similar in targeted fund-raising efforts and found that I even got a better response on letters I sent with a 32 cent stamp than I did with those that were sent as bulk mail.

I'm of the opinion that a congressional challenger could take a campaign fund of $200,000, earmark half of it for cable TV commercials, buy $15,000 worth of printed campaign hand-outs, recruit a hundred volunteers with computers that are willing to give him 20 days during the campaign to do mail-merge, spending the rest of the money on 32 cent stamps, and run a very effective campaign *without ever leaving his house* except for four of five TV debates. In fact, he might not have to even put on his pants but these four or five times during the campaign. No precinct walking, no candidate forums, no standing around grinning like an idiot, no luncheons, no rubber-chicken dinners, no signs to be stolen; none of this time consuming stuff that only serves to wear you out and get you pissed off.

He would couple this with an inter-active Web Site tied to a dozen or so politically- based search engines, and spend the rest of his time answering e-mail to voters who will probably vote. He would reach every voter likely to vote in the district three or four times with a personal *targeted* letter, his message will be seen on TV at least four of five times by every voter who watches TV, and *everyone* who goes to the polls would at least know who he is and at least something about his stand on some issues.

Now, I'm not the one to inaugurate this type of impersonal campaign, because I enjoy getting out and meeting people and hearing what they have to say, but it is an interesting concept. I also think the Web Site is here to stay, and I think we will see more and more electronic campaigning in the years to come.

ONE LAST REFLECTION

When I first talked with Barbara Collier about the possibility of running, she asked if I had ever thought of starting out a little lower in the food chain by running for a local office as opposed to a national office. I remember my exact words in reply. "Barbara, I am 60 years old. I don't have time."

Having met and gotten to know all the candidates in three counties, having appeared with them and watched their races, I'll share with you one last pearl. It is just as easy to run for the United States Congress, as it is to run for the School Board. Perhaps it is even easier.

10

WHAT NOW?

Perhaps the place to start is with the question I have been asked many times since the election, "Would you do it again"?

I might. But, it would be done in a whole lot different manner. As I said on countless occasions during the campaign, and in one of my TV ads, I'm not a politician. I am a businessman. I am not looking for a career. I have had my career. I have tried to put down on these pages the good, the bad, and the ugly. There was some of each, but the experience did not turn me off. Everything I have ever learned in life, I have learned by doing. Looking at the political process from inside the ropes one time is probably equal to at least two years of a secondary level political science education, although there are poly-sci majors out there who would disagree. I also have said numerous times during the past year that this was a one-shot deal; that I wouldn't put Sandy or myself through this again.

However, as I have attempted to put all this on paper, I have come to question just what was so bad that we put ourselves through? It was an experience. It was hard work, but it wasn't unpleasant. We met a lot of wonderful people and, basically we had some fun doing it.

Realistically, I probably knew that I couldn't win this election, but that did not hinder me from *trying* to win. There was a way that I could have pulled it off, but many things would have had to fall into place, and they didn't. First of all, I needed coat tails, and there were none. The Republicans did a masterful job of getting the message out to the candidates, but they did a terrible job of getting it out to the voters. Bob Dole ran probably the worst campaign that has ever been run by a presidential candidate, and the list goes on.

Beverly Kennedy, who ran against Deutsch twice and was defeated both times, told me early in the campaign that I should just try to build a political base in this race, not piss off Deutsch, and wait until 1998 when Deutsch would probably seek Bob Graham's Senate seat. Then I could probably win the open seat. I told her then that that is not my style. I did build a political base, but I probably pissed off Deutsch, and I *did* try to win. Besides, Graham has since announced that he is staying put, and so will Deutsch, so there will be no open seat.

Deutsch will be tough to beat in this district as it is now drawn. He has the political machine, he has the money, and he has a district with an overwhelming registration of Democratic voters. I have done my tour as a blocking dummy for the Republican party, and I am not suicidal. I would never climb behind the controls of a kamikaze aircraft, but I would have taken off with Jimmy Doolittle in his raid over Tokyo in 1942 because, although the mission was a very long shot, it at least had a *chance* and it was worthwhile. I think if I run again, I will have a chance, and it *is* worthwhile. If I don't do it, I hope someone like me does, and I will help them any way I can. I sincerely believe that we need to place citizen legislators in Washington who are there to get a job done, and then come home.

I plan to stay active in South Florida politics, help rebuild our local Republican party, and see what happens in the coming year. I also plan to stay very active in the Marine Sanctuary issue in the Florida Keys, because that is an issue that ultimately will affect the lives of a lot of residents there, many of whom have become our friends.

Deutsch said that he would support the will of the voters in the referendum on the Sanctuary, and he has already reneged on that promise. As everyone knows, two years can be a lifetime in politics. The following is an excerpt from an editorial, "Election Aftermath", that ran in the Key West Citizen two days after the election, *before Deutsch reneged on his promise to the voters:*

> *"Rep. Peter Deutsch should note well the groundswell of opposition in this county, at least, as exemplified by the remarkable toll of votes for first time candidate, Jim Jacobs and his ideas.*
>
> *Unheralded, underfunded, unsung, Jacobs gave a complacent congressman a fright.*
>
> *Imagine what he might have done had he had the full-court press backing of the Republican Party.*
>
> *Deutsch, who already is on record as saying he will support the wishes of the voters of Monroe County on the Florida Keys National Marine Sanctuary, should pay attention to what Jacobs' voters are telling him."*

The national and the state Republican party would have to want me to run to win and not to just fill the slate, and I would need the pledge of the money up front. The same goes for the power brokers, money bundlers, and the other major contributors in South Florida. I have proven that I can go head-to-head with Deutsch, or anyone else for that matter, and I can get votes. I will not go back to family and friends again for money, and I cannot afford to spend 90% of my time during the campaign trying to raise pocket change. *The Golden Goose has eaten all the grassroots.*

A word about Peter is in order, because I know he will read this. Peter treated me with respect, and I appreciate that, even though he may have done so out of fear of the unknown. He was quoted in the press as saying I was "a mystery man". He didn't know if I was going to dump a million dollars into the campaign in the final month, or what I was going to do. Well, when all one has is stealth, one uses stealth. We traded a few punches, but it never got ugly, and we certainly didn't sling mud at each other like his friends to the north. I'm proud of the way we conducted our campaign and I hope he is, too. I wish him well in the 105th Congress, and I told him so. To me, the only thing worse than losing this election would have been to win and go up there to a Democratic controlled Congress and have to sit on the back bench and listen to Gephardt for two years. That guy is really pushing the envelope on stupidity. But, if Deutsch stumbles, I'll be on him like ugly on Arafat. I am disappointed that he sold out the Florida Keys because I think that the welfare of 60,000 people should certainly transcend political ambition. But, he has his values and I have mine. I hope he doesn't take it personal that I did some butt-kicking in this book, because I didn't take it personal that he kicked my butt at the polls. I guess that's what they call "politics". Perhaps we should just look at it like we came to chew bubble-gum and kick ass, and we were all out of bubble-gum. Someday I want to ask him about that question he got in Big Pine Key that I don't think either of us knew what we were talking about.

This campaign essentially started when Bruce Brahe handed me a check for $100 in Crystal City, Virginia in 1995, two years ago. I think it fitting that this chronology of my campaign end with something Bruce gave me later. I don't know where he got it, but I know where I got it. I got it from him. It was written on the back of a bar napkin, and I saved it:

> *I could never be a "could be".*
> *I would rather be an "are".*
> *For a "could be" is a maybe*
> *With a chance of touching par.*
> *I would rather be a "has been"*
> *Than a "might have been" by far.*
> *For a "might have been" has never been,*
> *But a "has been" was once an "are".*

Bruce Brahe, FBI (Ret)
Hamburger Hamlet
Crystal City, Virginia 1995

EPILOGUE

◆

June–2002

B y the end of the 1996 General Election, the Broward County
Republican Party was in complete disarray. It had been held
together by duct tape and the simple fact that there was a presidential
election. Inertia carried us through it, but the contribution of the party
to the candidates was almost non-existent. Only two Republican candidates successfully defended their seats; Clay Shaw, the popular
Republican congressman, who had an opponent even less funded than
I, and Jane Carrol, the venerable, long-term Supervisor of Elections,
who ran on the promise that this would be her last race. Even with
that, she was almost unseated by a political unknown. Our standard
bearer, Bob Dole didn't help the party any more than the party helped
him. In fact, I received more votes in my congressional district than he
did. Simply put, we were on our ass to the point that I referred to our
monthly meetings as "The Monday Night Fights".

BREC elections are held right on the heels of the general election,
and a strong leader, Ed Pozzuoli, emerged as Chair, surrounding himself with an excellent executive board including Kevin Tynan, George
LeMieux, and a panel of "City Leaders" comprised of republican club
presidents and a few other political insiders. I had just formed the Central Broward Republican Club and was elected as the club's first president, thus making me a member of this informal, ad-hoc group. A key
player in this effort to rebuild the local party was Richard Ramos, the
paid Executive Director of the party in Broward County and one of the
most politically astute young men I have ever met. I had vowed to pay
my political dues and this became not only an excellent forum from

which to work for the party, but also to learn something about politics, something most people do *before* they run for high office.

Actually, many aspects of the political education of Jim Jacobs was more "suspicions confirmed" rather than revelation. One revelation was that BREC has a "school board mentality". During the campaign, I felt that I received very little help from the county party. I found this quite unsettling because, other than the presidential race, I headed the ticket in the 20th Congressional District. I didn't dwell on this because I had other things to worry about, and I just chalked it up to the fact that the consensus was probably that I had no chance to win and party assets could probably be better spent elsewhere. Well, most republican candidates in Broward have little chance of winning, but the fact is that the issues and events at the national level intimidate most BREC members. In fact my observations from up close are that issues above the school board level, such as those of state house and senate races are not easily grasped by the majority of the party activists. I don't mean to imply that such issues are too complex to be understood by the grass-roots workers; they just don't touch their everyday lives like the school board and county commission issues do, and therefore they tends to turn their efforts toward that which affects them.

Nevertheless, I faithfully attended the monthly meetings and worked hard at immersing myself into local republican causes such as "single member districts" for the school board that I personally couldn't care less about, but which I also knew were important to getting at least a few republicans elected in this notoriously democratic stronghold. This issue concerned dividing the county into seven school board districts with each aspirant to the board running from a particular district, rather than county wide. Hopefully, by accomplishing this, it was conceivable that one or more districts might fall out than had some sort of parity between registered republican and democratic voters whereby just maybe a republican could somehow get elected. We managed to get this passed, and then we managed to get a republican on the school board for the first time in many years.

An interesting sidelight to this was that before single member districts, each school board candidate faced 800,000 voters countywide instead of a little over 100,000 with the single member districts. In my campaign for national office, I only faced about 400,000 voters in my congressional district. Accordingly, just playing the numbers game, one could surmise that it was twice as hard to get elected to the school board as it was to become elected to the U.S. Congress.

Basically, I just kept a low profile within the party, gave up my presidency in the regional club I helped form as soon as it was possible to do so, spoke at a local candidate school, and would have been very willing to help any candidate that opposed Deutsch, but there have been no takers since 1996. Sandy won a seat to the Presidency IV, the state presidential straw poll, where we nominated George 'W' as the next president. I lost out in the lottery, but managed to get an appointment as a "City Leader". Probably the biggest thing that happened to me before the 2000 general election was that I landed an appointment to the Republican National Convention in Philadelphia as an Alternate Delegate.

The National Convention

It is fairly easy to get to the state convention, but the national convention is a whole new ballgame. There are only 1395 Delegates from the entire country, three from each congressional district, plus the same amount of Alternate Delegates. Many of these appointments go to elected party officials and major fund-raisers or heavy contributors. In Florida, the county chair, vice-chair, state committeeman and committeewoman from each county involved vote on the appointments, and delegate wannabes must make formal application, secure endorsements from party leaders, and then lobby these individuals for the coveted appointment. Since my district spanned three counties, there were 12 "selectors". The odds are so long in South Florida that most party-faithful don't even apply. I applied anyway. I think there were about fifty applicants in my district, all with heavy credentials. Also, both the

Chair and the Vice-Chair lived in my district, so there went two seats right there. There was even a chance to make a formal presentation on why one thought they should be selected. I availed myself of this opportunity.

My presentation was short and to the point. I allowed as how with 50 applicants for four seats they were about to piss-off 46 heavy-hitters. I made the point that I was the only applicant who had run for national office, and it followed that if they gave me one of the seats they could say to all the others, "Hey, Jim ran against Peter Deutsch. If you had run against Deutsch (who they all hate), we would have selected you, too. By my applying, I am actually trying to take some of the heat off you". I also told the panel that I just wanted to get to "The Show" one time, and that I would let someone else go in the future. I guess they bought it, because I received a call that evening informing me that I was an Alternate Delegate.

Let's talk for a minute about Delegates and Alternate Delegates. Alternates cannot vote at the convention, but Bush had the nomination sewed up as a result of the presidential primaries, so that vote was academic. The only other vote was on the party platform, and that had been pretty well cast in concrete by the time most of the delegates got to town. I certainly didn't agree with the abortion part of the platform, but a floor fight was not going to happen because we were there for one thing; to show party unity and to nominate George W. Bush. We would have four years to wrestle with abortion. Alternate Delegates sit behind the Delegates on the floor in the state's designated area. In Philadelphia, the alternates sat up in the first tier above the floor itself. Actually, we could see much better, and it was much cooler. Delegates usually swap credentials with the alternates so the alternates can get some floor-time, and even sometimes some face-time on national TV. This was especially so in Philadelphia because our seating was so much more comfortable.

Delegates and alternates can also register their spouses as "guests" who also have preferred seating. I was able to get Sandy into the alternate seating, and from there she even got some floor time. On one occasion she wore the credentials of Bill McCollum, a Florida House-member running for the U.S. Senate. I won't even try to describe the parties; they are non-stop and no delegate can even begin to attend them all. But, without a doubt, one of the proudest moments of my life was being there in that hall on the final night when the 100,000 balloons fell and George Bush was officially the republican nominee for president.

There are two other things I want to mention about the national convention. First, there is a misconception that the Republican Party picks up the tab for the delegates and the alternates. Not so. Everyone is on his or her own for transportation and lodging. Food is not a financial burden because there are so many parties, receptions, and hospitality suites, but the Florida delegation was even required to pay a mandatory assessment for a 24-hour a day hospitality suite and a breakfast buffet every morning for both the delegate and any registered guests. Having said that, I will also say that the state party staff mem-bers really busted their butts and everything provided by the party, even though we paid for it, was first class all the way.

The other thing is directed at future congressional candidates who might read this book. When I was running, the state party informed me that they would provide credentials to the national convention that was held in San Diego in 1996 if I wished to attend. At that time, since I joined the race so late, I felt that my time could be better served by staying home and campaigning. I figured that anybody I might meet out there who lived in my congressional district would vote for me anyhow, so I stayed home. However, what no one bothered to tell me, if indeed they even knew, is that congressional candidates, who are on the ballot, are allowed to speak for three minutes at the convention. Granted, this occurs during the first two sessions before the heavies take the podium, but it is still three minutes on national TV during the convention. Had I known this, I would have been there if I had to hitchhike

The 2000 Presidential Election

It had been sort of a long dry spell for me, working mostly on local issues, but with my attention at the national level. I predicted in the body of the book that the 2000 republican presidential candidate would be Lamar Alexander, but I had met 'W' at Presidency IV, the state convention and had come away with a favorable impression. I figured that a guy that had been spanked by the most beloved woman in America couldn't be all bad. I also talked in the book about the "dear neighbor" letter as a tool in getting out the vote and I was quite anxious to put the concept to the test.

Although the idea was spawned by Will Connelly, as I also acknowledged, I became its champion in the "City Leader" meetings, especially when it came to having the individual precinct captains write the letters personally, put their return address on them, and mail them with a regular thirty four cent stamp, rather than running them through as bulk mail. The theory was that if the recipient looked at the envelope and saw a personal letter from an address he recognized as that of a neighbor, that he would open it and, even seeing that it was political in nature, would probably read it. The message was quite simple, saying in effect to go vote. If I explained the need for a regular stamp once, I must have explained it carefully a dozen times, but sometimes one just cannot overturn the propensity of the Republican Party to screw up an iron ball. First, it was decided to send a form letter rather that a personal letter. Then it was decided to send a post card, rather than a letter. Then we had a mass addressing effort after one of the monthly BREC meetings, with those addressing the cards putting their own return address on the card, but sending it to a precinct on the other side of the county, thus losing any semblance of "dear neighbor". Just to make sure that the card got discarded along with all the other political bullshit and the junk mail, they were run through the bulk mail route.

Totally disgusted with the entire process, I demanded, and received 360 regular, self sticking thirty four cent stamps and wrote my own letter addressed to each registered republican in Precinct 36N, of which I am the precinct captain.

The letter is reproduced here:

Dear Neighbor,

Please take two minutes and read this. I think you will learn a few things about our neighborhood, and I promise I will not ask you for money.

*I am Jim Jacobs, and I am the Republican precinct captain (the politically correct name is Broward County Republican Executive Committeeman) for our neighborhood. Incidentally, the politically correct name for our neighborhood is **36N**. Our precinct is one of two located totally within the confines of Jacaranda Country Club. Ours is basically around the West Course. Over six hundred other precincts make up Broward County. This year our polling place is just across Broward Boulevard at the Central Park clubhouse. My job is to help Republican candidates get elected to public office. It's an elected position, and it pays nothing except a big dose of satisfaction knowing that I am an integral part of the greatest process on earth; the freedom to choose our leaders. That's what I really wish to talk with you about during the rest of my two minutes.*

Admittedly, being a Republican in Broward County is not much fun, because we are out-numbered by the other major party in voter registration by a margin of 2 to 1. There's not much we can do about that. However, consider this. In the 1996 General Election in our precinct, the Democrats out-gunned us 667 to 361 in Clinton vs. Dole, giving us four more years of Clinton and the resultant international embarrassment. But, in 1998 in McKay vs. Bush, they only won our precinct by 443 to 330, and of course, Jeb went on to win. When Republicans turn out to vote in 36N, we make a difference.

This year the State of Florida is nationally recognized as the swing state. The next president must have Florida's electoral votes to win. With only an eight (8) seat margin in the U.S. Senate, we desperately need to replace retiring Republican Senator Connie Mack with another republican, Bill McCollum. Broward is also nationally recognized as the swing county. Can 36N be the swing precinct??? So, you see, your vote does count, as Dick Cheney says, "Big Time!"

When Clinton won in 1996 in Broward County, the Democrats won by 180,000 votes. If they do that this time, Bush and McCollum will lose, along with many other fine local and state Republican candidates. If we can just hold that margin to 120,000 votes in Broward County, the good guys will win Florida, and Bush will go on to win the presidency.

Looking at it another way, consider 1960. JFK won the election because he received

> *ONE MORE VOTE per precinct in Illinois (8858 votes)*
> *TWO MORE VOTES per precinct in Missouri (9880 votes)*
> *THREE MORE VOTES per precinct in New Jersey (22091 votes)*

Without these 40,829 votes, Nixon would have won the election.

Good neighbor, that's my pitch. Please just go vote on November 7th. Never before, and never again will your vote be so important. If you have any questions, or just want to talk politics, give me a call at 475-9737. I'm also on-line at www.votejacobs@aol.com (what else). I'll be at our polling place all day on November 7th with palm cards. Please just walk up and introduce yourself and say hello.

The guy down the block,

Then I signed it "Jim". In light of what was to come, was that letter surreal, or what?

I must have received two dozen phone calls thanking me for the letter and promising to vote, where heretofore the person said they probably would not have voted without the reminder. In the days following the election, I probably received twice that many calls commenting on how I "nailed it". Who knows? Maybe we were the "swing" precinct. I do know we had an even bigger turnout in our precinct that when I ran four years earlier. But I am getting ahead of my story.

Election Day—November 2000

It was a complete cluster-fuck!

It was "Motor-Voter", people who had been registered when they applied for driver's licenses.

It was the DMV that failed to send the voter registrations to the Supervisor of Election for inclusion on the voter rolls.

It was people who have moved and had failed to inform the Supervisor of Elections, rendering their new precincts, and their old voter rolls incompatible.

It was people who had not voted in years, whose names had been removed from the rolls.

It was people who had never voted before in their lives.

It was people who didn't understand the ballot, and who were too stupid to ask for help.

It was a lack of Supervisor of Election infrastructure, i.e. telephone gridlock trying to reach election headquarters to verify registrations.

It was people who had requested absentee ballots, and then showed up to vote at the polls.

It was people who couldn't, or wouldn't read the instructions.

And it was a large group of people who were just too goddamn dumb to punch a hole in a piece of cardboard.

Contrary to what the liberal media, who jumped at the chance to spend the winter in South Florida, would have everyone believe:

What it wasn't were the voting machines.

What it wasn't was the ballot design.

And what it sure as hell wasn't was any attempt to keep anyone from voting. Anyone that claimed they had been disenfranchised did it all to themselves.

At the precinct I was working, I saw a poll worker collect about thirty names of people who could not be verified, have them promise to return after work, and then get in his car and drive fifteen miles to election headquarters to reconcile the problem. I saw poll workers trying to use their personal cell phones talking to headquarters personnel using *their* personal cell phones, trying to resolve problems.

And the butt of the whole South Florida fiasco was the Palm Beach County Supervisor of Elections, Theresa LaPore, who designed the infamous "butterfly ballot" in an attempt to help seniors with poor eyesight better use the ballot. What most news accounts failed to state was that both the Republican and Democratic Executive Committees of that county saw *and approved* the butterfly ballot for use in the election. This was before the sample ballot was printed very prominently in the local papers so that the voters could become familiar with it before arriving at the polls to cast their ballots. Thank god she was a Democrat. But, she still got a bum rap.

It might also be recalled that in the body of the book I became incensed when Dan Rather announced Bill Clinton the winner on 1% of the vote on my election night in 1996. I stated then that such practices should be banned, and then predicted that if allowed to continue it would bite somebody in the ass. Well, did it ever!

The Recount

First of all, what transpired in Florida was totally unnecessary. The fact is the Florida vote was a very close vote. Votes that close by law call for an automatic recount. This is very logical and proper. The votes should have just been recounted *by whatever method they were originally tabulated,* and then certified by the Secretary of State, and that should have been it. There is no doubt in my mind that the design of the butterfly ballot cost Al Gore sufficient votes to have cost him the election. I say this because it is highly improbable that some heavily democratic precincts in Palm Beach County would have gone for Buchanan, but voters must take a little bit of responsibility for their own actions. One just cannot enter a voting booth with their mind a complete blank. Since Florida ballots cannot be traced back to the individual, there was just <u>no way</u> to correct the problem.

Enter the lawyers. Hundreds of lawyers. If Gore couldn't prove that he had won, then he would just muddy the waters sufficiently, especially in the heavily democratic areas of South Florida, and maybe he would just get lucky and find a few more votes. Bush couldn't just sit idly by, so he sent in his hundreds of lawyers. Whenever that many lawyers clash, the result is preordained. The more impossible the circumstances, the more bizarre will be the attempted cure. But before we examine this bit of total folly, allow me to lead you through some things that were happening in Broward County that went largely un-reported, notwithstanding the fact that millions of words *were* gener-ated in an attempt by the press to describe and sensationalize the situa-tion.

First of all, while the legal teams were posturing and getting their "guns" in place, the ballots were sitting in an unguarded, non-alarm equipped building in perhaps the worst and most dangerous section of Fort Lauderdale, unless one wants to include Century Village. The fate of the nation is in the balance, and the ballots that will determine that fate are just sitting there in *unlocked* cardboard boxes with nary even a Rent-a-Cop on guard. I don't know who made that discovery, but Sharon Day, our State Committeewoman called me about ten P.M. on the evening following election day and asked me to take the 4 AM to 8 AM "watch" to insure that no one entered the premises. She promised that there would be two people on each watch, and that the drill would continue until the Supervisor of Elections came to her senses and moved the ballots to a more secure location. This latter statement was predicated on finding her, as she had *left on vacation that afternoon.* Can anyone believe that?

I showed up as instructed at 4 AM, and was met by a female fellow republican, who I did not know. She was dropped off by her husband, who was undergoing a nervous breakdown as a result of the events of the past 48 hours, having gone somewhat non-linear. I never inquired of any of the other "guards", but I was armed, not so much to blow away any democratic lawyers, although the thought was of some com-fort, but purely for self-defense in the crack-infested neighborhood. In fact, I think if I could have gotten Peter Deutsch out there with me, I could have brought him around to my way of thinking regarding gun control. Anyway, this "well regulated militia", of which our forefathers spoke so eloquently when framing the Second Amendment, remained on guard for two days until it occurred to someone in authority that the ballots just might be important and they were finally placed under heavy guard.

This occurred when the greatest legal minds in the nation managed to reach the worst possible reaction to a situation in which *any* action taken merely serves to exacerbate the problem. Their recommendation? *A manual recount.*

Somewhere, somehow a tiny bit of sanity manifested itself in the decision as to where to physically conduct the recount in Broward County. The county emergency management center is located in Plantation, Florida, a suburb of Fort Lauderdale, and is located about six blocks from my house. It is also probably the most physically secure building in the county, able to withstand category five hurricanes, and housing banks and banks of computers, phone banks, and even kitchen facilities. About 2 PM on the third day following the election I received a frantic phone call from Rich Ramos, the BREC Executive Director telling me to go there immediately, and to prepare to assist in the recount. The place was a zoo. Every sheriff's deputy in the county was there "guarding the ballots", notwithstanding the fact that they had not been guarded since the election except by the aforementioned well regulated republican militia. Also conspicuous were trucks and vans from every local and national news service, and sufficient satellite dishes and miles of cable to cover every single venue of the Olympics.

Scores of the faithful from both parties were filing in, having been snatched from their desks and out of meetings by the party leadership, each undoubtedly with the single-minded purpose of preventing those other bastards from stealing the election. Actually, the last statement is conjecture on my part, as I can only truly attest to my state of mind, which ran more to Pattonesque; the hell with keeping them from stealing from me. I'm going to steal it from them.

Each recount "team" consisted of two staff members of the Supervisor of Elections, one republican "observer" and one democratic "observer". Each republican observer had to be personally certified by another "known" republican as "known to him". I don't know what the democratic certification process was, although since they regularly vote dead people, it was probably somewhat more relaxed than ours.

The two "officials" would sit in the middle, and the two observers would sit one on each side of the two officials. Each team would sit as a somewhat isolated group. The chief official would pick up a ballot, look at it and declare it either, "Gore", or "Bush". He or she would then pass it to the other official and he or she would either agree or disagree. The observers were not permitted to touch the ballot, but the officials would hold it so that each observer could closely inspect the ballot. Once all four members agreed, the ballot would be placed either in the "Bush pile", the "Gore pile" or in the "contested pile". That sounds simple enough, right? Wrong!

When I walked up to the group to which I had been assigned, the other three were introducing themselves and shaking hands. I sort of snarled and said, "I'm not here to make friends. Let's get started." I didn't introduce myself, and I didn't shake any hands.

Anytime the officials declared a ballot a "Bush ballot", I didn't even look at it. I didn't care what it looked like. As long as the other observer didn't contest it, it was headed for the Bush pile, and I was not about to interfere with *that* process. *However*, if the officials called it a "Gore ballot", I would look at it for several minutes, having the official hold it up to the light, turn it over, whatever, and if there wasn't a hole you could drive a truck through, I would contest it, and it would go into the contested pile. There were also a few times I saw the official mistakenly put a Gore ballot in the Bush pile, or visa versa. If a Gore ballot wound up in the "Bush pile", I did not say a word. However, if the situation was reversed and a Bush ballot got into the "Gore pile", I would go berserk. After a ballot run was completed, I would have one of the officials hold the "deck" of Gore ballots up to the light, and if I could not see a hole completely through the deck where the punch for Gore should have been, it meant that in spite of my watching carefully, a Bush ballot had still managed to finds its way into the "Gore pile".

I describe this process to make two points. First, I have been asked, and I have also asked myself how I felt about deliberately trying to "steal" Gore ballots. First of all, I would never try to rig an election, vote twice, or do anything that was not completely within the law on any election. However, when a bunch of biased lawyers, biased judges, and biased courts place me in a situation such as I found myself, the only thing that really came to mind is another lesson my Dad imparted to me when I was young.

"Son," he said, "When you're standing on a rattlesnake's neck with your boot pinning it to the ground, it ain't no time to get religion."

The other, more important point is that, multiplying the above description of the recount process by hundreds of recount "teams", how could a manual recount possibly be more accurate that the count generated by an unbiased ballot counting machine?

It became even worse in the case of a real, bona fide defective ballot that the machine had actually thrown out. These were the ballots with "dimpled chads", "pregnant chads", "hanging chads", over- votes, where the voter had voted for both Gore and Bush, under-votes, where the voter had voted for neither candidate, and other irregularities that the "dumb" machine had refused to try to interpret, but which the "brilliant" courts had decided we mere mortals could handily decode. Had any state or federal election official, or any judge that assumed jurisdiction in this fiasco spent even ten minutes at a table as a member of a recount team, even the most biased diehard partisan would have seen immediately that a manual recount was the worst possible solution to an impossible situation, while the required machine recount was the only sane solution to the impossible situation. I honestly think that is all Katherine Harris was trying to do.

But, what if?

In spite of all the ridiculous things that happened in Florida during those 35 days, I honestly do think that Bush was the lawful winner. But, what if we hadn't held the line during those emotionally charged days when some of the best legal talent in the world was trying to snatch a Gore victory from the hanging chads of defeat. Can you imagine Gore's reaction following September 11, 2001 perhaps refusing to bomb Afghanistan for fear of blowing up their tree? And what about a guy named Lieberman trying to pull together a coalition of Arabs to go against a group of Muslims running amok? Or maybe SecDef Cohen might take his trophy wife to Saudi Arabia to host a cocktail party for King Faud and his dune coons while Secretary of State Madeline Half-bright danced around with her skirt up over her head? And, Ye Gods, Attorney General Janet Reno attempting to detain a thousand Middle Eastern immigration violators when she couldn't even deal with one illegal six year old boy.

As ridiculous as I make this sound, there are many liberals in this country who would support these actions because they have been supporting similar government fantasy for the past eight years. These people are too stupid to live in a free country because they have no clue how we became free in the first place, and they have no stomach for what it takes to remain free.

I think the American people dodged a bullet.

Peter Deutsch Revisited

The first time I ran into Peter following our race in 1996 occurred at the recount, which was, in fact held in our district, the 20th CD. He was there, as he should have been, generating some face-time on national TV and spurring on the democratic "observers". We chatted a bit, quite pleasantly, and he said, "Jim, come over here, I want to show you something." He placed his arm on my shoulder as we looked through a glass enclosure into the room where a hundred or so recounts were going on. He continued, "Just look at that. Republicans and democrats, sitting together and working together peacefully, trying to solve a common problem. That's what government is all about."

"Peter", I said, "It's peaceful because they made me check my gun at the door." "Dammit," he said, "You're never going to change."

The only other time I have seen him occurred during a series of locally televised Town Hall Meetings he was conducting around the county, not too long after the inauguration of Bush. BREC had decided to send out some "hit squads" to ambush him with "hard questions", and I was asked to be the sniper in Plantation. I refused the ambush as not being my style, but agreed to attend. I ran into him in the parking lot, and even helped him and an aide carry in refreshments. Once inside, I told him that I was there, not to ambush him, but to ask a question about "our" favorite topic, the 1993 income tax on social security benefits. He said that he appreciated the "heads up", and he did call on me when I raised my hand.

I stood and went over some background of our six or eight debates wherein I always beat him over the head with this tax and he beat always me over the head with my stand on gun control. I then asked him if during the past five years he had re-thought him position on this tax.

Surprisingly, he said, "You know, Jim, I have in fact thought a great deal about some of the things you said then, and I have come around to your way of thinking on that tax. Furthermore, I may even be willing to vote to eliminate that tax if it comes up again on a bill." Before I could thank him and sit down, he added, "Provided, of course, you change your position on gun control."

Well, I guess we seniors are just going to be stuck with that tax awhile longer.

A Parting Shot

In the book I was fairly lavish in my disdain for Bill Clinton, based on his actions as president during his first term in office. The writing of this took place before Monica, the impeachment, the USS Cole, and the mass pardons he granted as he packed the U-Haul with stolen White House "loot" as he went out the door.

Man, I wasn't even close.

APPENDIX

These are the "50 Questions You Had Better Be Able To Answer", distributed by the NRCC. Answering these questions helped me immensely in formulating my campaign platform and establishing my political ideology.

50 QUESTIONS YOU HAD BETTER BE ABLE TO ANSWER

1. **Why are you running for Congress?**

   There is a Revolution taking place in Washington, and I don't want to be late for it. The 104th started it and the 107th will just about complete it. The Great Society has been a dismal failure, created by politicians for politicians, and the country is almost bankrupt, and will be bankrupt if allowed to continue unchecked. A 'Business Approach *must* be applied to the Government. Lawyers, and certainly career politicians, alone are incapable of overhauling that which must be overhauled. Two-thirds of the 104th were businessmen with no prior political background and they have made an impressive start. Three-fourths of the 1996 Republican candidates will have strong business backgrounds and that is what it is going to take. I am willing to take that on if the voters will allow me to do it.

2. **What do you think are your main qualifications to serve in Congress?**

   Common sense; pure and simple. Conservatism is basically common sense, while liberalism seems to be some kind of abstract thinking where 2+2 might equal most anything. I have run major government programs in the private sector, met payrolls, competed for business and made a profit. I'm also an engineer and engineering is nothing but a logical thought process. Someone told me there are only 3 engineers in Congress. Well, I think there should be a few more.

3. **What are you objections to your opponent?**

    Well, to start with, he has been lying to his constituents about Medicare, he handed his retired supporters the biggest tax increase in history on their Social Security checks and he voted to send our troops to Bosnia, just for starters. I seriously doubt if there is a single campaign issue on which we will find common ground. This is one race where the voters are going to have a very clear choice.

4. **How are you going to win this race?**

    It's going to be tough because there are a lot more Democrats in this district than there are Republicans. However, all democrats are not liberals, and Democrats, and especially senior citizen Democrats are not stupid. I firmly believe that when they find out how they have been lied to by Deutsch, and Larry Smith before him, and study the issues, such as the *truth* about Medicare and the *truth* about Social Security that they will tend to vote common sense instead of the ticket.

    There are also a lot of Independents out there and I'm going to look a lot like an Independent. There is also a lot of population growth into West Broward and these young, affluent voters tend to be more conservative in their thinking. My job will be to get that vote out. Of course, this district is not merely composed of Broward County, where Deutsch has run strongly in the past, but also West Dade and Monroe County, where he tends to run less well. I am going to take the fight to him in all these areas.

5. **What does your family think about you running? Are they going to be involved in the campaign?**

They are delighted, and, yes, my wife will be involved in the campaign.

6. **How do you describe yourself philosophically?**

I'm a Type A personality with a strong sense of humor, which I think will be as asset in getting through the next eight months. I am also relatively hard-nosed when I need to be and ego has never been a problem with me. My stress quotient is high and like one of my heroes, Adm. Hyman Rickover, I tend to obey all orders....that I agree with.

7. **Have you voted in every election? Why not?**

I have voted in every election in the past ten years except 1994, and this has been with a job that has run me all over the world on a continuing basis. In 1994, I was on an extended trip in Washington and a critical event came up on election eve and I was not able to get back here.

8. **What is your net worth? Are you going to put your own money into the race? How much?**

I'm by no means wealthy, and what I do have is in real estate. I am trying to sell some property now in the Washington area and if I am successful in that I will put some of my money in, but it won't be a whole lot, because the only retirement I have is Social Security and these savings. I am willing to take a year out of my life campaigning and take on one of the worst jobs in the world as a citizen legislator for a 6 year period, but I'm not going to bet our golden years on the outcome of one election. Furthermore, my wife has had to go back to work after being out of the marketplace for ten years in order for me to campaign full time on this election.

9. **Are you going to release your tax returns?**

Sure, I have no problem with that.

10. **Aren't you worried that the House GOP is too extreme and in their haste to balance the budget is being unfair to those least able to defend themselves? The poor? The children? The aged? The infirmed?**

Who are you with, the Washington Post? I could talk all day on this subject. No, I do not think they are being too extreme. The Contract with America was a campaign promise to the American people and the American people responded with a mandate to carry it forth, and that's exactly what the House GOP did, with the exception of Term Limits. The only people screaming are the Democrats, who still don't have a plan of their own. What would be extreme to the point of criminality would be to do nothing and let Medicare go down the tubes, which is exactly where it is heading without a course correction, and this is according to Clinton's own Trustees. There is nowhere but in Washington can a 48% rise in Medicare payments over seven years be called a "cut". The Democratic demagoguery on this issue alone is one of the biggest lies ever perpetrated on the American public. And, you know what, the American people are not going to fall for it.

As for welfare reform, it is just that, "reform". The reformed program is work-based rather than a hand-out, it promotes a modicum of dignity where none previously existed, and it is not open ended. I think even most Democrats would agree that welfare needed a strong course correction.

Now to answer part of your original question: that involving "haste". I think there was a certain form of euphoria in Congress amongst the GOP, their having gained control of both sides for the first time in 40 years. Can you imagines being a galley slave, pulling on the oars for 40 years, when suddenly, overnight, you are transformed into that big guy with the whip counting strokes. After 40 years of not even being able to get a bill out of committee you now *control* the committee. I think this euphoria caused the GOP to take perhaps a bigger bite out of the absolute myriad of things that need to be corrected than they should have. But remember, the basic driving factor was that the new leadership was trying to fulfill their *promise* to the American people. Gingrich has taken the 'hit" for this, and the perception is definitely there that he is the "heavy". He personally told me not to try to defend him in my campaign. Well, I am defending him because he is a brilliant visionary. But, if the American voters will elect a Republican President, or if not, give the Congress a veto override, you are going to see economic progress and per capita prosperity such that this country has never seen before.

One parting shot on this. Basically, what the House GOP has done in the past year is nothing more than what Clinton "said he would do if elected". And Clinton and his minions have fought us every step of the way. More of the BIG LIE.

11. **Where do you stand on social issues? Abortion? Prayer in school? School choice? Home schooling?**

On abortion, I am pro choice. First of all, I don't know why this is a political issue, but I know it is. I see it as a moral choice. Perhaps as a political choice, it should be put to a National Referendum. And, while we're at it, let's don't give men a vote. Then, see where abortion lands. My problem is this. My whole platform is based on getting the government out of our faces and out of our pocket-books. Our country is based on the premise of freedom of choice. Our forefathers came here from England fleeing religious persecution and government oppression. How can I stand before you and say that I am for all of this but then turn around and say that, "Oh, by the way, if you want to have an abortion, you can't have one"? I am firmly against the government paying for abortions with taxpayer dollars, and I am against second and third trimester abortions, and I am appalled at the partial birth procedure. Nevertheless, I will not straddle the issue and I will not flip-flop to gain special interest support on this matter. I am pro-choice.

As for prayer in school, same answer! Besides, if any of you ever went through engineering school, you probably did one hell of a lot of praying. I certainly did!

School choice? Let me say here that I think the only idea in the history of this country dumber than sending our troops into Bosnia was the idea of school busing. 'Nuff said!

Home schooling? During the recent GOP Candidate School in Washington, my wife was talking with one of the other candidate wives, and she was nervous about this issue because she and her husband were home schooling both of their children and they were worried about the image that might portray to voters. I applaud her and I hope her husband wins. I have raised two separate families and I am very proud of the way they turned out. But, I have got to say that, given the state of our public school systems, were I in a family raising mode right now, I would seriously consider home schooling. When we are graduating high schoolers who can barely read the diploma they are handed, when SAT tests allow calculators to be used because many high school seniors do not know their multiplication tables, and when the Department of Education, in a recent announcement, removed all spelling standards from high school curricula because, "some children are *independent* spellers", I simply must cringe. Tell me how much better our primary educational system has become in the 20 years that we have has a Department of Education, and perhaps you can convince me that that Agency is not a great place to start the 105th Congress next major budget cut.

12. **How do you feel about the Republican race for President?**

I was a delegate at Presidency III, Florida's straw poll in November. I went there as an uncommitted delegate. My feeling is that the only criteria the Republican Party should use in selecting our candidate is *who can beat Clinton!!* With the possible exception of Ulysses S. Grant, Bill Clinton is probably the worst president this country has ever had. The sad fact is that he is charismatic and one hell of a campaigner. He is also "pretty", another sad fact that, unfortunately, that many voters tend to crank into their decision making process. Rep. Bob Dornan said it best when he said that the entire Republican slate is "charismatically challenged", himself excluded, incidentally. My feeling is, especially after meeting privately with him, is that Lamar Alexander can stand toe-to-toe with Clinton and debate him and, more important, can *beat him,* on the issues, on intelligence, on character, on experience, and, yes, on charisma. I am backing Lamar Alexander.

13. How do you view the Republican economic program? What parts do you support? What about the fairness of the tax cuts? and cutting Medicare to support them?

There you go again! a 40% increase in Medicare payments over the next seven years is not a "cut". The other LIE is that the reduction in run-away projected costs in Medicare from 10% per year to 7% in order to keep the Medicare program solvent is to be used to fund a tax cut is simply not true. The money paid into the Medicare fund has a "lock-box" provision that can only be used for block grants for the states to fund Medicare while the funds that support a tax come from the general fund. Furthermore, I do support a tax cut to the American taxpayers in order to pay back the 1993 tax increase, which was the largest tax increase in the history of the United States and fostered by the Clinton administration in order to spawn new lavish spending programs of very questionable value and serving only to broaden the deficit.

14. **What are your views on foreign policy? Do you support the President's plan to send peacekeepers to Bosnia?**

I don't think the United States should ever commit troops anywhere on foreign soil without a clear-cut National Interest. Then, in such a case, we should go in full force with the clear intent to win. The Gulf War was a prime example of where I stand on foreign policy, except that I think we should have finished the job.

As for Bosnia, this is an example of what not to do. There is no clear-cut national interest; it is a no-win situation. We are already furnishing 100% of the air power, 100% of the sea power and 100% of the supply effort. There is no defensible reason why we should put American troops on the ground and steadfastly in harms way. Clinton, by his naivety and pure political motivation is simply rolling the dice with American lives. He has reduced the title of Commander-in-Chief to an entry-level position. My opponent is no better because he voted to send in the troops. I am also very disappointed in the Republican Congress in allowing it to happen. This one is going to bite the United States in the ass.

15. **What are the most important problems facing our district right now? What would you do about trying to solve them?**

The problems facing our district are representative of the problems facing the entire nation. We are bankrupting generations to come. We are on course for the first time in my lifetime whereby our grandchildren do not have a chance to have it as good as the generation before them. Balancing the budget is certainly the No. 1 priority, but even that is not enough. We must create a surplus if we are going to meet our obligations to all our citizens in our two primary contracts with Americans; Medicare and Social Security. All the rhetoric about Social Security not being 'on the table" will be overtaken by events if we do not act to create a surplus now, because, like an elephant in the living room, it is just too big to be ignored forever.

Crime is another major concern to my district. We've got to get the liberal judges off the bench and get the liberals off the parole boards, lock up criminals and keep them locked up. Eighty percent of crime is committed by repeat offenders, usually multiple repeat offenders. Rehabilitation is out of the questions with this group. Furthermore, the death penalty can be a deterrent if only we will apply it. In Florida, with one of the largest 'death rows' in the country, we should have an "execution of the week" and show it on TV.

16. **Did you support all provisions of the Contract with America? Why? Why not?**

Yes. I support it for what it is; a start. There is much, much more to be done, however.

17. **Who is supporting your candidacy? Will the Christian Coalition be supporting your candidacy?**

Republicans, Independents and born-again Democrats will support my candidacy. I don't know if the Christian Coalition will support me or not. I am pro-child, pro-family, and pro-choice. I am also pro-gun. I'm not sure they can get their arms around all that. However, I'm not sure they will support my opponent, either. I will try for their support, but I cannot straddle the issues to get it.

18. **What kind of campaign do you plan to run?**

It will have to be largely grassroots, at least at first. This is because of money, pure and simple. My opponent will outspend me five to one. But I will go anywhere and talk with anyone. I'm not running for office; I am running for what I believe.

19. **Do you plan to use any negative style advertising?**

I would dearly love to run this campaign on the issues. However, knowing the type of person my opponent is and his penchant for lying to his constituency, it will undoubtedly degenerate to negativism. So be it. There is nothing I like better than a scrap.

20. **How much money is your campaign going to cost? How are you going to raise this money?**

It will cost every cent I can raise. I am going to raise it by spending at least 60% of my time fund-raising.

21. **Have you done any polling or seen any polling? What does it show? Do you plan to run a poll soon?**

I have not conducted a poll nor seen a poll. Until I have acquired some name recognition, I think a poll would be useless. The only thing polls are good for is fund-raising, so it almost becomes a chicken-and-egg thing. Furthermore, 80% of the voters make up their minds within two weeks of the election. I think polls are vastly over-rated. To test this theory, watch and chart the polls on the Presidential race, and then see how it comes out.

22. **How much time are you going to spend campaigning?**

Every waking hour.

23. **Realistically, what are your chances of winning?**

I am not putting myself through this with the idea of losing. However, realistically, some things have to fall into place in order for me to win. I have got to get my message out any way I can. I have got to create enough earned media to get a race going in order to attract money to keep it going. I have got to get the vote out by getting people that normally don't vote mad enough at what has been happening to this country under 40 years of Democratic majority to go out and vote. I have got to take the fight to my opponent because he will try to stay away from me. Also, it wouldn't hurt if Clinton gets indicted.

24. **Do you favor a cut in the capital gains tax?**

Absolutely! This is the dumbest tax ever levied on the American taxpayer. Furthermore, it is anything but a tax cut for the wealthy. Almost every person in this country with a household income of $50,000 or more is sitting on a pile of equity, either in their homes or in stock market investments. This is doubly true for senior citizens, who will continue to sit on their equity rather than give a third of it to the government. Cut the maximum capital gains tax to 19% and our national budget will balance in seven years. Cut it to zero and the budget will balance in five years and in seven years we will have the surplus we need to guarantee the solvency of Social Security and Medicare forever.

25. **What is the first bill you will introduce?**

That one!

26. **Which house committee assignments will you seek?**

I have been a government military contractor for over 30 years. I believe in a strong military and I basically believe in the military procurement system, although there is much needed room for improvement. I think I could bring a strong and valuable insight into the National Security Committee as a user of the system, as a businessman, and as an engineer. I would press hard for a seat on that committee.

I have also had experience in government contracts involving law enforcement and I have strong beliefs, convictions, and potential solutions for crime control in general and the war on drugs in particular. Drugs are driving the crime rate in this country and we need drug interdiction, drug law enforcement, mandatory capital punishment for drug dealers and then we need drug rehabilitation for drug users. I would also press hard for a seat on this committee.

27. **Do you support term limits? Which version?**

When I announced my candidacy I signed a self-imposed term limit of six years? Actually, the voters hold the ultimate term-limiter; the vote. But for some reason, the voters don't wield it and people in office tend to stay in office. Our Constitution sets forth a citizen legislature, but after four or six years it seems our citizens become politicians. I am not going to become a politician. It is also interesting to note that my opponent voted for term limits in the Contract with America. I submit that he knew that term limits would not pass, it being the only one of ten that failed in the House. I think he took a "freebie". Therefore, I challenge him to prove his sincerity in that vote by also signing a self-imposed term limit, as I have.

28. **Will you vote your conscience, or will you vote the will of the people in your district?**

On issues on which I am campaigning, I will vote my campaign platform, and the people that send me to Congress will know exactly what those planks are. On emerging issues I will tend to vote the will of the people in the district.

29. **Will you have a significant number of minorities supporting your candidacy? Are there any minorities in your campaign? Who are they? In what capacity do they serve?**

I will welcome support from any minority group and I will ask them to serve in any capacity for which they are qualified

30. **Do you support foreign aid? To Israel? To Egypt? To Russia?**

Yes, I believe in a certain amount of foreign aid, but I believe in less rather that more. I need to be convinced that the military and financial security of the American people is secured before I am willing to commit funds abroad for other than humanitarian endeavor. In many cases, I think the right answer in Washington is "No".

31. **What will you do to help poor people?**

The best way to help the poor is to help them help themselves. That is why I am in favor of work-based and time-limited welfare. I have worked every day of my life since I was twelve years old, even when I was in college with a wife and daughter. Education and training is the path out of poverty. I will support bills that make education and training possible and I will support jobs programs that are meaningful.

32. **Would you change food stamp requirements? Would you block grant them?**

Yes to both questions. I would support going from coupons to a "credit card' system and I would impose heavy penalties on food suppliers who allow unauthorized purchases with the credit card. I think this is the only way to keep food stamps off the black market.

I would block grant them for two reasons. First, I think Washington's role is to make the rules. Washington should not be in the business of writing checks on social programs. I also think it is infinitely easier for states to police fraud in these areas than it is for the federal government.

33. **How do you feel about campaign reform? Lobby reform?**

If I get beat in this election it will be because of money. PacMan Deutsch is one of the top, it not <u>the</u> top fund raisers in Congress. This is not too surprising because that's all he does, and he does it on taxpayer's time. Furthermore, most of his campaign financing comes from out-of-state. Virtually every sitting Member stays in by buying in because incumbency is very conducive to raising special interest dollars. I think every cent of non-Pac money should have to come from sources within the congressional district or from family. Pacs should be required to give a certain percentage of money to non-incumbents and television should be prohibited in all but Senate and Presidential campaigns.

It is not untypical for a congressional campaign for a House seat to cost one million dollars? This is the price to pay to get one of the worst jobs in the world that most people wouldn't touch with a ten foot pole and that pays $133,000 per year. There is something dreadfully wrong here. No, I think the candidates should walk the neighborhoods, meet the people, hear what they have to say, tell them where you stand on issues, go to Washington if they find you worthy, and then come home in a reasonable length of time to get something done that the people sent you there to do. This may sound idealistic, but I think that is what the founding fathers envisioned, and they wrote one hell of a document.

The same is basically true for lobby reform. Lobbyists serve a useful purpose. A Member cannot possibly be on top of every issue that comes to a vote. I would look upon lobbyists as essential to explaining intricacies in a Bill to my staff and me. Lobbyists will have access to my office, but it will be for my education in casting an informed vote and not to curry favor with junkets, ski trips and lavish dinners.

34. What will you do to bring jobs to your district?

I am running as a pro-business candidate. I have been a businessman for over thirty years. I understand what it means to have a "real job" rather than feeding at the public trough as a career. I will meet with any company representative who seeks my support in bringing jobs to my district and I will seek out the representatives of any company known to me contemplating a corporate move or the establishment of an extension of the business in Florida. It seems logical to me that a company looking for a site would lean toward a congressional district in which the sitting congressman is 'one of them".

I also have an extensive background in government competitive procurements. I have won my share and I have lost a few. While I would never try to influence a government federal procurement, I would go out of my way to make it known to federal procurement officials that I am carefully watching the procurement process to insure that there is, indeed, a fair and level playing field where companies within my district are involved.

35. **What should be done about illegal aliens? Affirmative action?**

Illegal aliens should be deported immediately upon discovery, pure and simple. Our country was built on immigration, *legal immigration*. Our immigration laws are probably the most liberal immigration laws in the world, perhaps even too liberal. With such liberal immigration policies, anything less than strict enforcement of these policies will serve as a beacon to an undesirable class of people that are fleeing their own failed nation and arrive on these shores assured of the Democrats imposed right to 'humanitarian aid" (welfare funds). Bill Clinton is not Noah, and the United States is not Noah's Ark.

Affirmative Action is another Great Society disaster. This country was built on free enterprise and competition. With Affirmative Action came a distinct stifling of both. I am a corporate officer in a small, Hispanic, woman owned, disadvantaged business enterprise. All we need to do is file with the Small Business Administration in order to qualify for set-aside government contracts that we can get with little or no competition and at prices that would be totally uncompetitive in the free market. Thousand of minority businesses have done just that and are literally raping the government procurement system. We have chosen not to file for such status, even thought we are fully qualified to do so and meet all the requirements. Why? Because it is not right. Everyone in this country should be guaranteed an opportunity. No one should be guaranteed an outcome. We are currently bidding on a Navy contract in this district worth $13 million dollars. We are in competition with several "large businesses" and, by filing for 8-A status, as this scam is known, we could probably have had this contract 'set aside', possibly even awarded to us as "sole source' as the only qualified 8-A firm available. We chose not to go this route because this is not right. Such is not in the best interests of the government or the American taxpayer and Affirmative Action is a scam and should be exposed. If I am elected to Congress, I will, in fact, do everything in my power to expose this Great Society scheme as another of a long list of liberal ploys that flies in the face of everything that has made this country great; free enterprise and healthy competition.

36. **Do you support a flat income tax? The consumption tax? A national sales tax?**

I support something other than we now have, but I'm not sure at this point what that change should be. The criteria for tax overhaul must be "fairness". The cornerstone of my campaign is to get the government out of our collective faces and the IRS is a great place to start. Any fair system that eliminates, or at least, greatly reduces the need for IRS has appeal. A flat tax has appeal in its simplicity and "apparent" fairness. Likewise, a national sales tax has appeal in that it will tend to capture the "underground economy", not the least of which includes billions of dollars in drug money. However, there is a real chance that with a national sales tax and a surcharge of fifteen to twenty percent on every purchase might cause an accompanying national "sticker shock" leading to a national downturn in retail sales with predictable impact on the economy.

Assuming that the 104th Congress will succeed in dealing effectively with Medicare, balancing the budget and welfare reform, my prediction is that the bane of the 105th Congress will be to deal with overhaul of our tax system. The issues facing the 104th Congress have the dubious necessity of 'having to be done". Tax reform falls into the category of 'should be done". Being arbitrarily less urgent, tax reform should be carefully studied, exhaustibly debated, and hopefully agreed to in a totally bipartisan manner and within the best interests of the taxpayers as to fairne

37. Do you support drug testing of employees by businesses?

I support letting businesses make that decision. I think enabling legislation should be in place to allow individual business to implement drug testing policies should they so desire but it should be left to the discretion of the individual company with three exceptions; Businesses receiving government contracts should be required to have in place a government approved drug-free workplace policy as should businesses involved with the handling and transportation of hazardous materials and businesses involved in public transportation.

38. Do you support the use of polygraph machines by private business? Do you support their use by the government?

The use of polygraph machines are susceptible to misinterpretation and are, if made mandatory, are a violation of the Fifth Amendment. I would not support their use by business, even on a voluntary basis by the employee. Having said that, I feel there is one exception, as there is to every rule, and that is in the area of national security. I would support the use of polygraphs in screening for high level security clearances of Top Secret and above, and for the periodic updates thereof. Employment in these sensitive areas is a privilege, rather that a right, and individuals have the right to seek other employment should they elect not to undergo polygraph testing. The Ames case certainly comes to mind.

39. **Would you support an increase in minimum wage?**

Only that the increase is indexed to inflation.

40. **Should there be federal laws on drunk driving? A national minimum age for drinking?**

Again, get the federal government out of my face! Again, there is an exception. If a person is on active duty in the military service, he or she should be allowed to drink in any state by presenting a valid military ID card. If they are old enough to go into combat, they are old enough to drink if they so desire. Otherwise, the states make their own laws, including enforcement of their drunk driving laws on military personnel.

41. **Do you support gun control? In any form? Should the assault weapon ban be repealed?**

No. Not in any form. The assault weapon ban should be repealed because that is a form of gun control. The 2dn Amendment enacted in 1791 gave the people the right to keep and bear arms and it is unconditional. What people tend to either forget, ignore, or never knew in the first place, is the reason that our forefathers gave us this right was not to combat crime, but as a defense against local, state, or government police power run amok. As a strong anti-crime advocate, if I thought gun control had *any* chance of deterring crime, I might give it a second thought. I don't, and I won't. I own a handgun, I have a license to carry it, and I do on occasion. If I have any indication that local, state, or federal government is about to run amok, I will buy an assault weapon…and I would use it if threatened.

42. **In what ways are you different from House Speaker Newt Gingrich? Won't you be just one more vote for Newt?**

The biggest difference is that I don't have his ego. I think he is brilliant and a great visionary. I am smart and a visionary. This translates to the fact that he is quicker that I am, but I get there. It probably also translates to the fact that I tend to think through an issue more than he does before I speak. We are both irreverent.

No, I will not be another vote for Newt. I am my own man. I will not go into Congress owing Newt or anyone else except the voters that send me there.

43. **How would you dispose of nuclear waste?**

In precisely the same way that the government is currently doing; by storing it in the safest place possible. I have this information lawfully via previous government contracts, but it is classified and I cannot elaborate on it.

44. **Are you in favor of spending more federal money to clean up hazardous waste? What about the Superfund Appropriation?**

The EPA is the epidemy of a government agency running amok and ignoring the requirement for which it was created. The EPA has 39,000 employees grinding out regulations that constrict law abiding citizens and businesses in every way imaginable, but have done almost nothing to complete the job that that it was chartered to do in the first place. It is to the point that you or I cannot go down to Home Depot and buy a gallon of paint and take it home to paint the bathroom without breaking several EPA laws relating to transporting hazardous material. And, God help you, if you cross a bridge on the way home because then you have broken several more laws. Or how about a man named Kelly Herstad of Duluth, Minnesota, who took his car into a refinery in 1952 for a 'hot oil flush" and had to spend $10,000 this year to clear his name with the EPA. For this story, there are a thousands more like it.

The Superfund is an abysmal failure. Superfund is 15 years old. Of the 1300 sites designated for Superfund cleanup, only 75 have been removed from the national priorities list, an average of five sites per year. Some of these were even removed because it was decided that clean-up was not even needed. This sorry record comes at a cost of more that $60 *billion in public and private monies.*

Some states, like the state of Minnesota, have taken the matter into their own hands, so disgusted are they at waiting for federal action. Minnesota has cleaned up more sites in 12 years that the federal government has in 15 years.

In current EPA regulatory law,. passed in recent years by the Democratic congress, the EPA requires businesses to spend as much as $500 million to avoid one hypothetical case of cancer. This is not an actual case of cancer in a real person. This is a theoretical case of cancer based on EPA computer models. If ever there was an agency deserving of top to bottom reform, if not total abolition, it is the EPA.

45. **What can be done to improve the quality of education in your district? Do you support more federal spending to improve public education? Goals 2000?**

As stated in Question 11, above, the first thing we need to do, as with everything else, is to get the federal government out of our public education system. We have the best colleges and universities in the world, and they are either run by the state, or they are run by the private sector. Conversely, we have a primary educational system that has become almost subservient to the Department of Education, again fueled by liberal legislation, and this system and the *survivors* of it, have slipped far down the list as compared with other civilized nations. One doesn't have to be a rocket scientist to figure out where the problem lies. The Department of Education would be at the top of my political hit list, to be zeroed out, and its functions relegated back to the states and administered by the local school boards.

46. **As a congressman, what would you do about crime?**

I touched on that in 15 above. Basically, I would introduce and support legislation that champions law enforcement and the rights of law-abiding citizens, rather than the rights of criminals. I would support Exclusionary Rule Reform, whereby evidence gathered in good faith may be used in a court of law. For decades now the Democrats have been looking out for the rights of criminals and giving them "get out of jail free cards. Well, we're not playing monopoly; we are going to play hardball. Under Democratic criminal pampering

- the average time served for murder is 6.5 years

- the average time served for rape is 3.5 years

- the average time served for assault is 1.5 years

- 80% of inmates have more than one past conviction

This revolving door must be shut and locked.

We need an effective death penalty and an end to the endless appeals.

We need violent criminal incarceration. When 6% of the criminals commit 70% of the crimes, the answer is not prevention or rehabilitation. The states that get serious about locking these people up and throwing away the key will get more funds to build more prisons. The Democrats worry about prison overcrowding. I worry about me, and you, and my family, and I don't care if they are stacked ten deep, I want them off the street, especially that 6%.

We need more block grants to police departments. The problems in North Dakota are not the same as those in North Brooklyn. It is for the local law enforcement officials to say how the money will be spent.

47. **Will you debate your opponent anywhere, anytime, and on any subject?**

Absolutely! But it won't happen. He will not get on a stage with me.

48. **What experience have you had that qualifies you to be a congressman?**

Let's define "congressman". There is a new breed in the revolution that is taking place in the House, and which will spread to the Senate. I am inspired by that new breed because they are not career politicians: they are businessmen who have agreed to become citizen legislators for a period of time in their lives and who are committed to cleaning up the mess that has been made by career politicians, most of whom are lawyers, under 40 years of Democratic control. What qualifies me for *this* House is over thirty years of successful business experience, an abundance of common sense coupled with the analytical capability of an engineering background, uncommon street smarts, a military background that was extensive enough to give me an understanding of the military mind and short enough that I didn't get 'hooked', and an absolute fire in my gut that tells me that, once we have brought this government under control and turned it back to the people in the form of lower, *fairer* taxes, more jobs, a stronger economy, and more security for our seniors and more hope and opportunity for our working men and women, and an overall, better way of life for our citizens, that maybe then, a congressman can be looked upon with a modicum of respect. That's not the way it is now.

49. **Why are you a Republican? Have you always been a Republican?**

I could no more be a Democrat than I could be a car thief. Conservatism is common sense—nothing more. You don't spend money you don't have. You honor contracts you do have. You don't habitually redistribute the wealth.

I think Dick Gephardt said why I am a Republican better than I can. He recently said in a speech before the House that, "Those who have been fortunate in the lottery of life have a moral obligation to share that fortune with all others".

Well, first of all, life is not a lottery, far from it. Success come from hard work, risk and reward, and a whole bunch of other factors, including a certain amount of luck. Our Constitution says that all men are created equal. It does not lay out what will or should happen beyond that. Other than paying his *fair* share of taxes, and contributing to charity *as he sees fit,* a person who makes it in life is under no obligation, moral or otherwise, to share any of it with others. Nor should it be taken from him and *given* to others in the form of redistribution of wealth. Even if a person should win the Lottery, are we to think that he should share his winnings with everyone around him? Of course not! The idea is absurd. Gebhardt is absurd. And the liberal mind-set is absurd. That is why I am a Republican.

Needless to say, yes, I have always been a Republican!

50. **What do you think about the GOP Medigrant program? Are you at all worried that it is unfair to the elderly or to children living in poverty?**

What would be unfair would be to let Medicare continue to fly in the face of Clinton's own Trustee's warning that the program will be bankrupt by the year 2002 without strong corrective action. I think the "Medigrant" program, as you choose to call it, is a sane, rational corrective action that will save the program. The most salient provision in the program is the stipulation that health care recipients may elect to keep the same program they have if they so choose, and are not required to switch to a managed care program unless they wish to. What could possibly be fairer than that? As far as the "grant" provision, I think it is the charter of the federal government to make the rules, but it is the charter of the states to administer the program. With Washington writing the checks for all 50 states, it is an absolute invitation for massive fraud, which is exactly what we have. I think that just by administering the Medicare program at the state level that we will see enough reduction in fraud, just because of proximity, that the savings may well be more than the deficit that was predicted. It is entirely possible that such could lead to a reduction in individual premiums, once this effect has had time to take hold.

I guess the biggest thing that is upsetting to me, and it should be upsetting to a lot of people, is that all the Democrats have done is to blast the plan while *they don't even have a plan!* That's why there has be no debates; there is nothing to debate.

As to the second part of the question, am I worried that the program is unfair to the elderly. This silver hair is not pre-mature. I am 61 years old. I'm about to be elderly. Furthermore, I paid into Social Security for 43 years and I paid into Medicare for 30 years. I want it and I will need it. There is no way that I am going to go to Washington and support any program that I don't think is fair to the elderly. Who can best represent the seniors of this district? Someone who is 4 years away from qualifying for Medicare and Social Security or someone who is 27 years away from qualifying. Who should you trust?

THE SANCTUARY—THE VIEWS OF THE CHALLENGER

by Jim Jacobs

(Published by the Key West Citizen as an op-ed Editorial on the weekend before the election, November 3, 1996)

I have not spoken out on the issue of the Florida Keys National Marine Sanctuary (FKNMS) for a number of reasons, the most salient of which is the very nature of the job for which I am a candidate, your representative in the U.S. House of Representatives. This is a local issue and, as a resident of Broward County, I do not have a vote on the sanctuary referendum. Furthermore, as a candidate, I must forswear upholding the will of the people within my constituency when I am elected. However, the question came up in a candidate interview with this paper, and it came up again in a debate on Big Pine Key that same night, and I feel compelled to respond, as I did on both occasions. I have requested this forum from the Citizen for my amplified response, and they have graciously consented.

The fundamental difference between our form of government and other forms is that our government is based on each individual having unrestricted rights. With our vote, we sometimes allow our local, state, and federal legislators to restrict our previously unrestricted rights. This is usually done to preserve a peace or to promote a common good. The basic cornerstone of our Constitutional form of government is that *we will not allow restrictions on our previously unrestricted rights by any person we cannot remove from office with our vote.* This concept is so simple and so basic that you should probably read it again to make sure you agree with me on this crucial point.

The primary sworn responsibility of every legislative leader is to protect and uphold the Constitution and to represent the constituents who elect him or her. One of the basic jobs of a legislative leader, whether local, state, or federal, is to insure that the rights of the citizenry are not restricted any more than is absolutely necessary and to specifically insure that those rights are not restricted beyond what the legislative body has allowed. Another key element of our constitutional form of government is the provision that the administrative agencies, such as NOAA, are beyond the control of the voters and they are not to be given the purely legislative power of restricting previously unrestricted rights.

In 1991, Congress enacted the Florida Keys National Marine Sanctuary Act, at the behest of Rep. Dante Fascall, who sought to protect and preserve the Living Coral Reef south of the Keys.

Congress enacted the FKNMS Act because they were told that the residents of the Florida Keys *wanted* a sanctuary, and the sanctuary they wanted would prohibit oil drilling and protect the reef tract from damage. It did not include 2800 square miles of largely international waters and essentially all of the Florida Keys. My understanding is that Congressman Deutsch has since reiterated that contention *of the expanded Sanctuary* before Congress in committee, and that he has been a leading proponent of the Sanctuary in its expanded form ever since his election in 1992, actions that clearly indicate an abrogation of his responsibilities as the guardian of the rights of the residents that he is sworn to uphold, because Rep. Deutsch has not only taken sides, but he has emerged as the leading flag-waver of outside special interests seeking to totally encapsulate the Keys with a national preserve. Even more disturbing, he has driven a wedge into his constituency in Monroe County by total lack of leadership in failing to articulate the options open to the voters of this county and by failing to explore those options with his constituents. Lastly, he has illegally delegated his legislative power to an administrative agency, which, in itself, is a ground for recall.

I make this charge because, as I have traveled the Keys in this campaign, I have seen neighbor against neighbor, coalition against coalition, environmentalists against business and property owners, and Upper Keys against Lower Keys. What is abundantly clear to me is that everyone *doesn't* want *this* sanctuary, as it has evolved. Thus, it comes down to a vote. This vote is unbinding on the future of the Sanctuary, but it *is* binding on your permanent loss of right to vote for your legislative leaders, because a YES vote transfers the power of restricting your rights within the Sanctuary to an administrative agency (NOAA), which is beyond your right of recall. As I said in the second paragraph, sometimes, *through votes*, we give the government the right to restrict us. But we do not pass on those rights of restriction to persons we cannot remove from office with our vote.

Deutsch was recently quoted in these pages as saying that he would support the will of the majority in this straw vote. Well, it *is* an election year and he has *not* been re-elected. Nevertheless, he has already abrogated his responsibility to the people of Monroe County by taking sides in probably the most important vote that any of you will ever cast if you plan to live out your lives in the Keys, as I know a lot of you intend. As the challenger, I am under no such lawful restriction to restrict my opinion.

By way of background, I have made my living as an engineer in, on, and under the ocean for the past thirty years. I have held contracts to perform underwater construction projects, clean up oil spills, and provide open ocean and harbor clearance salvage services for the U.S. Navy worldwide. Included in this was the un-stranding of the M/V Wellwood that went aground on the Pennekamp Reef in the mid-80s. I have also held contracts supporting U.S. Navy operations in Key West for the past twenty years. I know the ocean and I know the waters of the Florida Keys. With over thirty years as a government contractor,

I also know the government bureaucracy, as well, and *I don't necessarily trust them.*

I remember the first time I went to Disney World. It was in the early eighties and I had been working for the government as a contractor for about twenty years. I will never forget how impressed I was with the logic of the physical plant, the efficiency of crowd control, the morale and cheerfulness of the employees, and the smoothness of the whole operation. Then it suddenly occurred to me that the *federal government didn't have anything to do with it.* If it had, nothing would have worked, they would have been losing money, and the taxpayers would have been subsidizing it.

What I see with the FKNMS is a once well-intentioned reef tract restoration project that has mushroomed into a 2800 square mile area of unbridled restriction reaching from seawall to 300' water depth, an 800 page management plan with open ended powers, undefined and unstated user fee schedules, a disturbing propensity for levying fines on unwary, or unlucky, violators, and an absolutely frightening power to regulate and restrict runoff from adjacent private property into the Sanctuary over which the property owner may have no, or limited, control, and which may well have a tremendously adverse effect on property values in the Keys. What I also see is a huge bureaucracy already moving into place, an enforcement cadre diverted from crime prevention on the streets of the nation to harass sport fishermen and other legitimate users of your waters, and a mentality dedicated to raising funds to pay for this bureaucracy through fines, user fees, and permitting fees, a virtual pipeline straight into your pocketbook. What I don't see is any sign of scientific effort to define and quantify the problem(s) with the reef or any recommendations pertaining thereto.

The Congress still must ratify the FKNMS Act. This will probably occur early in the term of the 105th Congress. Hearings should be held on the matter. If I am your elected Representative *hearings will be held.* That is why your vote on the FKNMS on November 5th is so important. Although the vote is only a "straw", or non-binding vote, the results will be the *only* indicator available to Congress of the wishes of the residents of Monroe County.

I think everyone reading this should go back and read the second paragraph of this article again. The only way your inalienable rights can be taken away is if you *vote to give them away*. Once you do this, you have no recourse because administration of the FKNMS will be totally in the hands of a bureaucracy which you not only cannot control, but against the decisions of which, you have no recourse. There are *three* obvious choices that you should be voting on next week; YES, I want the FKNMS; NO, I don't want the FKNMS; and YES, I want the FKNMS, but it should be confined to the reef tract only, as originally conceived. Unfortunately, the people of Monroe Country will not be allowed to vote on the latter option because the framers of the referendum chose to play hard-ball and to go for "all or nothing". I suggest you give them *nothing*! Furthermore, every community leader and every business leader in the Middle and Lower Keys, who has actually studied the final Sanctuary plan is asking you to vote NO!

If you vote NO on this referendum you will not have voted away your rights. If you put me in office, I will stand before Congress and say that the FKNMS, in its present form, is not what we need. I will then meet extensively with *all* the residents of Monroe County and we will articulate a plan that marries our vision for the future of environmental protection with a preference for limited government and local control to preserve and protect our reef and I will get these collective ideas before the Congress, and the State legislature, in such a manner that we can accomplish the goal of protecting our Reef without the need to sign over our inalienable rights to a federal bureaucracy over which we have no control, and which is already demonstrating a tendency to run amok.

If you vote YES, the FKNMS will be ratified in its present form. I will still represent *all* the people of Monroe County, but there will be precious little that I can do to protect your rights because you will have voted them away and you will have *no* chance of getting them back.

This issue should never have come down to this, but it has. I think a YES vote is far too high a price for you to pay to protect and preserve *your* reef.

Jim Jacobs
Plantation, FL

INDEX

-C-

0-595-23528-X